A PREPPER'S
GUIDE TO SHOTGUNS

A PREPPER'S GUIDE TO SHOTGUNS

HOW TO PROPERLY CHOOSE, MAINTAIN, AND USE THESE FIREARMS IN EMERGENCY SITUATIONS

ROBERT K. CAMPBELL

Skyhorse Publishing

Skyhorse Publishing books may be purchased in bulk at special discounts for sales promotion, corporate gifts, fund-raising, or educational purposes. Special editions can also be created to specifications. For details, contact the Special Sales Department, Skyhorse Publishing, 307 West 36th Street, 11th Floor, New York, NY 10018 or info@ skyhorsepublishing.com.

Skyhorse® and Skyhorse Publishing® are registered trademarks of Skyhorse Publishing, Inc.®, a Delaware corporation.

Visit our website at www.skyhorsepublishing.com.

10 9 8 7 6 5 4 3

Library of Congress Cataloging-in-Publication Data is available on file.

Cover design by Tom Lau
Cover photo credits: Chiappa, Marocchi, Mossberg, iStockphoto

Print ISBN: 978-1-5107-2483-9
Ebook ISBN: 978-1-5107-2484-6

Printed in China

CONTENTS

PREFACE

For decades now, many of which I've spent in law enforcement, I have relied upon the same proven equipment for my self-defense and emergency preparation needs. That equipment consists of Colt 1911 pistols, Remington 700 rifles, and Remington and Mossberg shotguns. After seeing many changes in law enforcement through the years, I realize that each new piece of equipment we were handed required more training. To operate a radar unit the officer must understand not only how to set the radar up, but also take a class heavy on Hertzogs and the like. We now have computers in every vehicle in most jurisdictions giving us critical access to important information, but they took training too.

With firearms, the new class of polymer-frame handguns were another addition that took acclimation. They are lightweight and reliable, which is beneficial considering all of the other gear officers now carry—but oh, were they different from other semi-autos and the revolvers before them.

Among all these changes, the pump-action shotgun has remained the same. These are simple firearms that require a minimum of training. Today there are more dangerous felons than ever, and many of them are well armed. The chances of facing gangs of criminals or even terrorists is higher than ever. Night battle is another consideration that must be accounted for—and not just for law enforcement, but also for the average citizen.

Crime comes in all shapes and sizes. Most of us think about the types that make headlines: armed robberies, car jackings, home invasions, rapes, and other physical assaults. But those aren't the only emergencies that happen to people. Natural disasters such as wildfires, hurricanes, tornados, ice storms, and earthquakes can leave communities without running water and power for weeks on end. Increasingly on the minds of some is how to be prepared for an even bigger emergency, such as a foreign attack that takes the country off-grid and into hysteria. It is with a nod toward all of these that this book is written, for to be fully prepared to face the worst, no tool in your bag of preparations can perform so many tasks as the shotgun.

The emergency shotgun is a rack-grade firearm that comes up shooting no matter what. It can stop an attacker bent on taking your life or that of your loved ones, stop someone from taking over a shelter needed to survive, and put food on the table when protein is scarce. It can protect your less-perishable food stores from vermin and theft, and it can launch special munitions that signal for help or temporarily incapacitate an attacker. No matter who's behind its trigger or what's in its chamber, a shotgun's barrel is one into which no adversary wants to stare.

You have picked up this book because you have thought about how to prepare for the worst—good for you! I encourage you to digest all this book offers and others on the subject. Seek out training from professionals who specialize in survival tactics. Always, continuously be aware of your surroundings and think about what might happen in the realm of things not good, think about where you are, where you might be, and how you'll respond. If that response involves a shotgun, then you'll be better prepared for having read this book. Good luck, good shooting—and may you never have need to use what you learn here.

—*Robert K. Campbell*

INTRODUCTION

When I first began shooting shotguns, I pursued small game. I'd had considerable time behind a .22 rifle, graduating from my first single-shot to a self-loader. Moving to a harder-kicking shotgun (harder-kicking compared to the .22 rifle), in the beginning, under the careful supervision of my grandfather, I fired a few shots from a .410-bore; I was awed by the power of this inoffensive shell.

That single-shot, bolt-action Mossberg served well. Once I had the okay to take it into the field, I was impressed with the shotgun's ability to put game on the table (after all, prior to my time with that .410, I had been helpless against running game, and I'd hunted only squirrel and the occasional bedded rabbit with the .22 rifle).

The shotgun added new dimensions to the hunt. With the Mossberg bolt-action .410 over my shoulder, I headed into the forest and began regularly taking small game. Running game fell, and bedded rabbits were not torn up badly when taken with a headshot. My grandmother patiently prepared this game for the table. The meat was very good and healthier than the table fare to which most of us have become accustomed. Advancing to flying game such as dove and quail, however, I was limited by the performance of the .410-bore shotgun, and so I restricted my shooting to the ranges at which I felt I could connect. I never patterned the gun on paper, because no one told me to.

When my grandfather knew I was ready, I graduated to a Mossberg 500 12-gauge shotgun and larger game. The pump-action wore a 28-inch barrel with a Modified choke. I began to appreciate quiet walks in the dark to the hunting field, the dew on the ground, and the sun coming up over the fields in the morning. I became successful as a wingshot. The Mossberg 500 took quite a number of doves and quail and became my favorite shotgun, one I used for years—I cannot imagine being happier with a firearm! Although I am much better schooled today, the knowledge I had at the time regarding how to use that shotgun and my understanding of its performance in the field made me a happy young man.

After graduating from high school and attending college, I began to realize how precious time was. I missed the simple part-time jobs I had once worked, as I took on full-time work during college. Studies took most of my time night and day, and the remainder was filled with a job that had real responsibility. My time in the field became almost nonexistent. I still had only one shotgun, that Mossberg 500, but I could not imagine needing another.

On entering police work, I was exposed to the riot shotgun. These were Remington 870 shotguns with 18-inch barrels and Cylinder chokes. Training was slim to none with this shotgun; teaching young cops to use these firearms just wasn't high on the list of priorities, and what practice did exist was at the academy and limited, if memory serves, to five shells fired at a seven-yard target. But since we had all grown up as hunters, the pump-action itself was as familiar as the backs of our own hands. That was a good thing, because even without training, we were expected to be able to use the shotgun well since even though these firearms were considered to be a last resort, they were also ultimate "problem solver."

On my own, I took one of the agency shotguns out a few times for practice and was quite impressed. Twelve-gauge buckshot generated what seemed four times the recoil of the Winchester No.7½ field loads I had used in bird hunting. Too, the pattern on the Remington was much wider than what I had been used to from my 28-inch Mossberg sporting shotgun, but it was more than adequate at short range.

In our squad cars, the Remington 870 was kept at the ready, armed with a few Remington Power Piston buckshot shells. On a number of occasions, I saw the damage this combination was capable of inflicting—it is always a firearm to be respected.

As time went on and I saw more of this shotgun in action, I realized its versatility. Power, reliability, and speed to an accurate first-shot hit are all virtues. Yet the riot or tactical shotgun is often underutilized. I think this is because of a lack of training with this specific type of shotgun. Even with training, there is often a lack of understanding regarding recoil, and recoil is the single greatest impediment to properly learning to use any shotgun. Still, the shotgun stands alone when it comes to personal defense and responding to crises momentary to long-standing, small to catastrophic. It will protect your home, the farm, and hard points of refuge. It can save the life of you and your loved ones, either in defense or because it secured some life-saving protein. It is my hope that this book provides you a way to acclimate to the ways and wiles of the short-barreled defensive shotgun so that it becomes a trusted part of your emergency preparations—because, when you come right down to it, the shotgun is the one tool, perhaps more than any other, that is essential to being prepared for the worst.

CHAPTER 1

A BRIEF HISTORY OF THE SHOTGUN

The history of shotguns coincides with men beginning to use firearms, but the differences between the rifles and shotguns of those long-ago years were blurred; both solid shot and multiple balls used in many of both early firearms. Typically, a solid single shot ball was used for longer range work, while multiple balls were used at shorter ranges. For example, artillery pieces used cannon balls for breaching doors and walls. Canister or multiple ball shot, on the other hand, was used against opposing troops at shorter ranges.

Since the invention of firearms, the question has been: A single large shot or multiple small shot?

The first firearms had much in common with the today's specialized scattergun. They were handguns and muskets, though some, at least by modern definition, were what we'd call shotguns. The common military musket, for instance, did not have a rifled bore. This was to enable easier loading of balls, as the bore tended to become quickly fouled with spent powder. Some type of patch, usually made of linen, paper, or even hog grease, was wrapped around the ball to smooth its loading.

Often, a soldier on guard duty or involved in controlling crowds would have his musket loaded with more than one ball. Indeed, there might be up to three balls, which in total were lighter than the common musket ball, and the powder charge might even be lighter. There is evidence that American patriots killed in the Boston Massacre were done in by muskets loaded with multiple shot.

FIRST CAME THE BLUNDERBUSS

The shotgun slug, left, offers a formidable striking area.

Over time, firearms were developed to suit specific purposes. The need for long-range accuracy was one such purpose, and, eventually, barrel rifling created the first rifles. The shotgun, meanwhile, maintained its smooth bore for use with shot loads.

Among the most important predecessors to the modern shotgun was the blunderbuss. Typically shorter than a rifle, it was designed to use a load of shot and be handled quickly. It was closer to the modern fighting shotgun in many ways than were the fowling pieces developed later.

The blunderbuss featured a flared muzzle that permitted rapid loading of the powder and shot charge. Some were flared only slightly, while others were flared aggressively with a trumpet-like muzzle opening. With such a design, the blunderbuss was a deadly firearm in tight quarters and was often used for area and perimeter defense. It was also used to guard prisoners; it was a fixture in the Tower of London, for example. A guard armed with a blunderbuss might exhibit control over a half-dozen prisoners simply because of the threat of the awesome effect of the firearm's charge.

The blunderbuss was also used by the military as a cavalry weapon. Early horse pistols were effective just past saber range, and they were simply pointed (rather than aimed) by the mounted troops using them. Their single heavy ball could drop a war horse in its tracks when delivered in the kill zone.

Shot charges, on the other hand, were used against mounted soldiers, and the blunderbuss was much more effective here. At short range, its effect on the enemy was unquestioned; the shot quickly spread and was of little use past conversational range. A short version of the blunderbuss was originally called a "dragon." It was, basically, a pistol-sized blunderbuss, featuring a thick stock and barrel. This early firearm eventually became known as the "dragoon" and lent its name to an entire class of soldier. The dragoons were the heavy-shock troops of their day.

FOWLING PIECES

The early shotguns closely followed the pattern of rifles and pistols in development. The ignition system, for instance, progressed to flintlock and then caplock. The overall configurations of rifles and shotguns were also similar, though the shotgun typically had a heavier stock and the belled barrel of the blunderbuss.

In America, per my research, the blunderbuss was not as popular as the musket. The longer ranges typically encountered in the New World did not lend themselves well to using the short-range blunderbuss. The first true shotguns, however, were ideal for hunting and personal defense in the American wild. These sporting shotguns were known as "fowling pieces." They had little in common with the blunderbuss or dragoon.

The first fowling pieces featured a long barrel and used the flintlock firing system of the common musket. Very few double-barrel shotguns were designed and used in America, their primary drawback being their expensive production costs and retail prices, the latter of which was usually beyond a working man's salary.

As hunting skills progressed beyond the capabilities of the firearms available, it was the need for a better hunting shotgun that led to some of the most important developments in firearms history. The flintlock rifle often proved accurate, but was limited by the slow ignition time of the flintlock shotgun. In answer to this problem, noted inventor Alexander Forsythe developed the percussion lock. Instead of using a flint to strike a spark that ignited a small amount of powder in the gun's "frizzen" or "pan," which then ignited the primary charge and fired the shotgun, the Forsythe lock used a percussion cap that set upon a brass nipple. When struck, the cap transferred fire directly to the full powder charge.

The percussion cap changed the firearms world, leading to the development of successful breechloading firearms, repeating firearms, and practical single- and double-barrel shotguns. While fowling piece examples date back to the time of King Henry VIII, practical shotguns owned by working men didn't become common until the late 1700s. The Forsythe lock and the breechloading firearms of the 1830s, then, were important to the development of all firearms, but particularly the shotgun.

BRASS, PAPER, AND PLASTIC

While self-contained cartridges of linen, powder, and balls were developed for rifles and handguns, the single most important advance in shotguns was yet to come: The shotgun shell.

A brass shotgun shell.

With the advent of breechloading firearms, this was now possible.

There was much experimentation before the shotshell form recognizable to a shotgun user today was finally realized in the 1870s. Those first shells were primarily made of brass and differed from a rifle cartridge in that the rifle cartridge featured a bullet crimped into its case but protruding, while the shotshell contained the shot charge completely within its body, the nose of the shell having some type of cover to contain the shot. Usually, this was some type of paper wadding or board material. Used in single-shot and double-barrel breechloading shotguns, these shells weren't subjected to travel through a magazine or the pounding of multiple firings, such as with today's auto-loaders and pumps. The construction of these early shells, therefore, did not have to be as sturdy as our shells today are.

Following those first brass-hulled shotshells, paper shells of a tightly wrapped, cardboard-like material were invented, also in the 1870s, and these remained in regular use for almost a hundred years, to the 1960s.

The brass shotgun shell featured one of the first central primers. The powder charge was contained in the lower part of the shell. To keep the powder charge and shot payload separate, a divider called a "wad" was developed. Many types of wads were used, including paperboard, or what we would call cardboard today. Other materials included cork, felt, and leather, although the paper wad was the most common. On top of the wad was the shot load, with small shot used for fowl, larger shot for bigger game, and large balls known as "buckshot" for warfare or deer hunting.

Along with advances in hull material, there were also advances in primers, with some of the first modern primers containing both the priming compound and an "anvil." When struck by the firing pin, the explosive material in the cup is crushed against the anvil, producing ignition of the powder charge. Today, a few makers offer paper shells in their sporting or vintage lines, but these are a much more highly developed form of those originals. They are a charming

The author dissected this old paper hulled slug load. It wasn't particularly rigid.

diversion to use in a classic shotgun. Polywad offers the 2½-inch 12-gauge shell that must be used in vintage shotguns, and Federal Premium still produces its famed Gold Medal Paper Target Load shotshells, a favorite among the trap and skeet crowds.

Other advances made in the shotshell included modifications to the wadding or wad, which resulted in better shot pattern consistency. Felt, cork, and cardboard wads were used. Paper shells started to give way to plastic shells by the late 1960s; the tendency of paper shells to swell from moisture, as well as feeding problems in self-loaders, eventually led to their general demise. Although classic paper shells are still available, the majority of shells today are made of plastic, with brass heads and plastic wads. In loading a primed, empty shotshell hull, first comes the powder charge. On top of that is seated the "wad." A modern one-piece wad generally consists of three components:

1. The bottom of the wad, the part sitting on top of the powder charge, is the "powder wad." This acts as a gas seal for the ignited powder charge.
2. Above the powder wad is the "cushion," sometimes referred to as the "piston." It compresses when the shell ignites, helping to minimize shot deformation during ignition.
3. On top of the cushion is the shot "cup." This contains the shot charge and holds it together until the shot exits the barrel, preventing the

shot from contacting the sides of the barrel as it transitions through it. The shot cup is designed with "fingers" or "petals," vertical splits in the shot cup that allow the wad to open as the shot charge exits the barrel. This enhances pattern consistency. Today, there is a great deal of specialization in shot cup development. Some loads have been developed to give tight groups. Others, such as the Spred-R by Poly-wad, quickly and uniformly spread a shot payload at close range.

Gamebore still produces quality waxed paper shells.

This is the now universal roll-and-fold crimp used with shotgun shells.

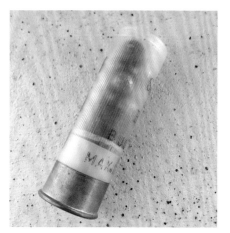

Modern economy buckshot loads utilizing a wad with a fingerless shot cup don't throw a great pattern, but they offer affordable practice.

Every gauge is available in different lengths and power levels. This is the .410-bore.

MORE THAN ONE SHOT

As shotshells were developed to provide greater versatility and power, the shotguns that fired those shells also saw a great deal of development. The invention of brass shotshells, for instance, gave way to the production of repeating shotguns. Few of the early repeaters were successful, but they were quite interesting. The Roper shotgun was one. It featured an enclosed magazine and fired from an open bolt!

Oddities aside, most authorities agree the first successful repeating shotgun was the Winchester 1887. This robust shotgun was a lever-action with a tubular magazine under the barrel. Adapting this rifle-like magazine to the shotgun was a great step forward in their development; the lever-action shotgun gave frontier lawmen an immediate advantage, with more than two shots at their disposal. Another shotgun type was coming, however, one that changed the shotgun world and is still the top choice among many shotgunners today: The Winchester 1893 pump-action.

The Winchester 97 made a mark on shotgun history.

The pump-action is one in which the fore-end is moved along rails to the rear, which unlocks the bolt and ejects a spent shell. Moving the fore-end back to its front-most position moves a fresh shell from the tubular magazine under the barrel up into the chamber, while closing the bolt and making the gun instantly ready to fire again. With its multiple-shot magazine, the Model 1893

Winchester's military 00 Buckshot load is the standard by which all others have been judged for more than 100 years, ever since its use in the Moro Rebellion in the Philippines.

had plenty of reliable firepower. It set the standard for shotguns today. The perfected Model 1897, the follow-up to the 1893, is also still in use in the game fields. During the hard-fought actions in the Philippines, it was the Model 97 that outshone both the .38 revolver and, to a large extent, the .30-40 Krag rifle. Twelve-gauge buckshot was the only reliable stopper available against the Moro people of the Moro Rebellion. The Winchester 1897 was also used to great effect in the brutal trench warfare of World War I. the shotgun has been used for close-range defense of positions, for assaults, and for cavalry action for practically the entire history of US Armed Forces.

BATTLE READY

Shotguns for use in trench warfare were highly developed. The Winchester 1897, for instance, was fitted with a bayonet lug and heat shield. This iteration is referred to as a "trench gun." This short-barreled shotgun, with a barrel length of 18 to 20 inches, later became known as the "riot gun." It was used in World War II by the United States on all fronts, and by partisans and guerilla forces in Europe not only during WWII, but in the Spanish Civil War before it.

The shotgun did have its limits in battle, as its effective range is short, but for taking on groups of soldiers in bunkers and in dense woods and jungles, the shotgun was ideal. In hand-to-hand street fighting, it proved unequaled. One of the military consultants for this book noted that the Claymore mine that has been praised for its effectiveness is basically a remote shotgun with a similar effect (not to underrate the Claymore's six-foot-high and 50-meter-wide dispersion, of course).

In the years since WWII, shotguns have been used in practically every conflict. Usually, they are pump-action shotguns such as the Winchester 1897 and 1912, Remington 870, and Mossberg 500 and 590. However, it has

The Winchester 1887 was a sensation in its day. This is a modern replica from Taylors & Company Firearms (www.taylorsfirearms.com).

been reported that the British used the Browning A5 semi-automatic shot-gun to great effect in the Malaya conflict against communist insurgents. Various Browning A5 models, along with Remington's clone of the A5, the Model 11, were also used for guard duty during WWII.

The Winchester 1897 saw its greatest baptism during the US campaign in the Philippines, from 1899 to 1902. The opposing Moros were tough and resolute warriors. They sometimes bound themselves with leather to prevent blood loss in the event of a deadly wound. The Colt .38-caliber revolver was a complete failure in action against these men.

It is less well-known that the .30-40 Krag in its original loading was also less than effective against the Moro. I think the failure of this cartridge in the Moro rebellion contributed to the replacement of the Krag rifle and the development of an improved loading; the Springfield .45-70 carbine, for instance, was often used at guard posts, as the huge lead bullet would be effective against a single adversary. But a weapon that was truly treasured for short-range fighting during the rebellion was the Winchester 1897 loaded with 00 Buckshot.

The pump-action shotgun was also used in forays against Mexican bandits, gaining a sterling reputation before WWI. There was considerable technological development during WWI, with both light and heavy machine guns and flame throwers developed for use in trench warfare. The Americans brought their Winchester Model 97s to the war. Issued primarily to scouts and forward units, in addition to guard posts, this shotgun was an excellent performer in close-quarters fighting. One account tells of a soldier shooting German grenades that had been hurled over the trenches out of harm's way. In fact, the shotgun was so effective that the Germans filed a diplomatic protest against this "barbaric weapon" (never mind their use of mustard gas).

The shotgun was kept in the Army arsenal and used again during World War II. Period photos show the shotgun typically used by the point man in Marine and Army teams, particularly in Pacific jungles. The shotgun was used continually and was particularly effective in Vietnam in close-range jungle combat. Although use of the Winchester 97s continued through Vietnam, other pump-action shotguns such as the Winchester Model 12, Savage pumps, and the Remington 870 were used as well.

To this day, the pump-action shotgun is still an important part of the military service arsenal, used for door breaching, close-quarters combat, and for guarding prisoners. Door-breaching shotguns use a special stand-off muzzle attachment. The barrel is placed against the latch of the door, and a special heavy-metal charge is fired against the door. The shock breaks the lock or hinge and the door may be opened.

Shotguns continue to be used in combat. A correspondent tells me that, on some missions, as many as one in ten soldiers will be armed with a shotgun, usually a Mossberg 500 or Remington 870. US military studies have shown that the shotgun has the highest probability of successfully making a fast hit on a human target of any shoulder-fired weapon.

Limited magazine capacity and penetration are factors that force the shotgun into specialized, short-range operations. In the high mountains of Afghanistan, for example, the shotgun is practically worthless. However, when the time comes to clear caves, it is a critical weapon and the shotgun is used everywhere for guarding prisoners. Harking back to the reputation of the blunderbuss, no one, nor a large group, wishes to rush even one guard armed with a shotgun.

Note: An interesting development in combat-ready shotguns is found in the adoption of the Benelli M4 Super 90 shotgun by the US Marine Corps. Some are also in the US Navy S.E.A.L. inventory. These are possibly the most reliable semi-auto shotguns ever built.

Modern shotgun loads include special riot-control loads called "flexible batons."

THE SPORTING SIDE

For civilians, most shotguns in use prior to 1900 were either single- or double-barrels. The double-barrel shotgun can have either two triggers, one for each barrel, or with a single trigger that will operate a second firing mechanism for the second barrel after the first barrel has been fired. The side-by-side barrel configuration is the most common in Europe, while the over/under style reigns in the US The most common double-barrel design is the type that hinges on the receiver, with the barrels levering down for loading. Side-by-sides have also been produced with sliding barrels that move forward for loading, and various latches that allow the barrels to move to one side or the other.

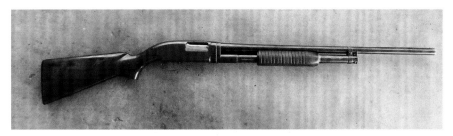

Stevens pump shotguns were reliable and affordable, and many still serve. This is the archetypical sporting shotgun.

In double-barrels, the barrels are not exactly parallel to each other, rather they are "regulated" so that the shot load of each barrel will converge at a certain point with the load from the other, most often at 30 to 40 yards. As an example, my old Stevens 311 shotgun lands Lightfield slugs in the same hole from either barrel at 20 yards.

With double barrels having fixed chokes (i.e., they do not have modern screw-in chokes), especially side-by-sides, one barrel is usually choked tighter than the other. An open Cylinder barrel may be used for flushed birds, as an example, while the other, more tightly choked barrel at Modified would take the longer shot at a bird that got away after the first flush. Short-barreled coach guns intended for personal defense are usually supplied with fixed open chokes in both barrels.

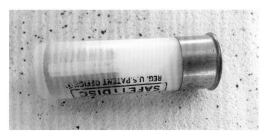

This load attempted to duplicate the legendary "roll of dimes" load with flat metal discs.

The earliest shotguns had external hammers that had to be cocked by the thumb for each shot. These remain popular among sporting vintagers, cowboy action shooters, and collectors. But a new design that employed the break-open action

These are all-copper, high-penetration slugs developed a generation ago.

to cock the striker was a great advance in break-action shotguns. These became the most popular double-barrels, and the hammer-fired or "rabbit-eared" shotguns became a novelty.

This load uses a light plastic projectile for safe close-range practice.

Lever-action shotguns were introduced during the cowboy era. The Winchester 1887 was important, then, because it was the first successful repeating shotgun. Their use of a tubular magazine in particular was a huge advance because, for the first time, shotgunners had more than two shells at their disposal before reloading.

The lever-action shotgun is still available today, though its popularity is mostly found among Cowboy Action competitors. Rossi,

Double-barrel shotguns are not as popular as they once were.

Chiappa, Taylors & Company, Century Arms, Henry, and Marlin all produce versions, mostly in 12-gauge and .410-bore.

The pump-action, upon its introduction, quickly replaced all others in popularity. Although the double-barrel shotgun remained popular for some sporting use, the pump-action became the favored shotgun for police and military use. (Even so, my research indicates that the double-barrel shotgun was used by some law enforcement agencies well into the 1970s; two controlled shots delivered with speed cannot be underrated.)

Early pump shotguns lacked a trigger disconnect. As long as the trigger was depressed, the shotgun would fire when the action was cycled. While this allowed for very fast shooting, one has to wonder how accurate such shooting would be. I have reenacted the action with a modern Winchester 1897 copy and also with an original 1950s Winchester 1897 shotgun—and the experience is awesome! Firing below eye level, with the shotgun under the shoulder and keeping the trigger held down while racking the action, you could probably plow down several attackers at close range fairly quickly. I suppose a wolf pack or a pack of feral dogs might warrant this type of self-defense technique. Still, without a trigger reset, you may not be in control as well as you would be with a more modern shotgun. John Moses Browning developed self-loading actions for the handguns, rifles, and shotguns that were based on using the force generated by a fired cartridge. Locked-breech and straight-blowback-operated handguns were among those developed, although Browning also experimented with rotating barrel and gas-operated handguns. Rifles used recoil-operated and gas-operated actions, while shotguns used both recoil-operated and gas-operated actions; the action ejected the spent shell, cocking the action as it did so, and then loaded a new shell.

The Browning Auto 5, sometimes simply called the A5, was the first successful self-loading shotgun and, arguably, the most successful semi-automatic shotgun of all time. The John Moses Browning design was regarded by the inventor as his best firearm.

The A5 is a popular sporting shotgun with tremendous appeal on every level. Special short-barreled versions were developed for military use. At one time, the FBI kept Browning A5s in its inventory for dealing with dangerous felons. Some of these wore standard full-length barrels as their tighter choke gave agents the ability to range out further than they could with the average riot gun.

HISTORY CONTINUES

The story of the shotgun is an ongoing one, with new developments occurring regularly. While the shotguns used a hundred years ago are still effective for home defense, more advanced shotguns are available. The challenge is to design a shotgun with the fast handling and natural point of the traditional shotgun, while offering improvements in functionality, sighting, and magazine capacity. What the future holds is anyone's guess, but I suspect that more development will focus on the purely personal-defense configurations, such as

Kel-Tec's KSG is perhaps the most advanced shotgun developed.

Pump-action and the double-barrel shotguns remain in service, albeit in forms often much modified from their originals.

the Kel-Tec KSG. Tactical shotguns like the Robar custom versions will also find new popularity, and sporting shotguns may become lighter in some versions. Stay tuned.

CHAPTER 2

CHOKES, LOADS, AND PATTERNING—CHOOSING THE RIGHT TOOLS FOR THE JOB AT HAND

The shotgun is a versatile game-getter. It is suitable for taking small game, such as squirrel, and with the proper load and choke, the same shotgun may be used for high-flying ducks and Canada geese, as well as for bigger game like boar and deer.

Clean-burning, affordable shells are essential for sporting use.

Why talk about hunting in a book for emergency preparation? Because when you think about such preparations, you need to think not just about immediate, day-to-day emergencies or criminal encounters, but the long term. What would happen if your neighborhood, your state, or even the nation had its power grid disabled? Whether it's by natural disaster such as an ice storm, wildfire, earthquake, tornado, or hurricane, or because of an attack on US soil that takes out critical infrastructure, you could be without power for weeks and months. Refrigeration won't be an option then, so hunting daily for your protein might be the only way to survive.

Because the shotgun is such a multi-purpose instrument, it is important to understand the differences in shot and loads for the shotgun. You should have a clear understanding of your emergency preparation needs before you choose a shotgun, and you should also understand the differences between sporting and personal-defense use before a purchase is made and you begin training.

THE SCIENCE OF CHOKES AND LOADS

Since the tasks of game taking and personal defense are so different, so must your shotgun and the loads you choose to shoot through it be different.

You can do a pretty good job with one shotgun that accommodates different chokes and, perhaps, a change of barrels. A shotgun's "choke" is simply defined as a constriction of the barrel. Most shotgun barrels have the same internal dimension throughout their length, until the end of the barrel near the muzzle. The end of the barrel, the last couple inches, is where the constriction or choke begins. The choke simply squeezes the shot payload into a smaller column, which improves patterning performance and allows greater flexibility in addressing targets at various distances.

Personal-defense shotguns do not usually have a choke at all; most are bored with an open Cylinder constriction. Others have removable, screw-in choke tubes of various constrictions, including the FNH FN SLP Tactical model and the TriStar TEC-12. Screw-in choke tubes allow the shooter to switch constrictions anywhere from the most open Cylinder to Super-Full.

When choosing the choke for your shotgun, the game is the guide. Quail rising quickly require a relatively open choke and a wide pattern; only a few pellets of small size need catch the bird for a quick, humane kill and an edible bird. A tighter patterning load of larger shot, on the other hand, would leave you with a shredded bird and a dinner plate full of as much shot to chew on as meat.

Birds taken at distance, such as doves, pheasants, and many waterfowl species, would require a tighter choke, along with a shot size appropriate to the game (more on shot sizes to come in the next chapter). Deer and predators such as coyotes and wolves are usually shot at longer range and also demand a tighter choke. When hunting large animals, the goal is to center the entire load, such as buckshot (a buckshot load is typically a few very large pellets compared to many smaller pellets in a dove load), in a tight spot, rather than counting on a few pellets to do the business. Turkeys also require a super-tight choke, so as to make a quick kill and do minimal damage to the meat.

The question of which load and choke today finds its answer in the technology of shotshell construction and your own experience in the field. For instance, you should know that when hunting, too open a pattern may result in too light a hit and a failure to anchor the game with enough shot. Too tight a pattern can result in misses. It is imperative the choke and the load be chosen wisely by consulting experienced hunters and authorities in the field, and the shotgun should be patterned on a paper target in order to measure the proper choke. Let's talk about that.

CHOKE CONSTRICTIONS

As stated before, chokes come in a range of constrictions. In order from most open to most constricted, the common choke sizes are Cylinder, Skeet (and sometimes Skeet 1 and 2), Improved Cylinder, Light Modified, Modified, Improved Modified, and Full. A variety of Extra-Full chokes in various degrees of tightness are available for turkey hunters and some waterfowl applications. Cylinder is practically worthless past 20 yards. Others are useful well beyond 50 yards.

SHOTGUN PATTERNING—YES, IT'S IMPORTANT

Patterning a shotgun before you head afield or begin to practice with it for personal defense is a responsibility you should take seriously. Patterning gives you a visual realization of where your shotgun's load of pellets will hit at a given distance, as well as how those pellets are dispersed.

Why does this matter? As hunters, we always want to make the quickest, most humane kill possible. That quick kill is your first priority, but there are other considerations as well. In the case of game animals intended for the table, we also want to do minimal damage to the meat, and with predators, fur-bearers, and other huntable species that aren't common table fare but are destined for taxidermy or a fur coat or blanket, we want to minimize damage to the pelt. Patterning helps determine what shotshell loads and chokes have the best chance of accomplishing these things, provided you make the accurate, well-placed shot.

Patterning also matters because different shot sizes, loads, and shot material all affect how any given payload of shot distributes through any given choke constrictions—and not all loads will pattern well or consistently through any particular choke. For instance, a target load of No. 8 from Brand A may pattern very well through a Beretta Modified choke, while a comparably loaded shotshell from Brand B may not. That Brand B load may do very well through a Browning Invector Modified choke, leaving the Brand A load in second place. And you won't know any of this until you pattern your loads and chokes.

Patterning isn't hard, but it takes some time. The first thing you'll need is knowledge of the game you intend to pursue and the common loads for that game recommended by ammunition manufacturers; many, if not most, modern shotgun loads intended for game have pictures of the game they're suitable for on their boxes, so this isn't as hard as it sounds. Next, you'll choose a couple chokes and loads that you anticipate will be appropriate for your planned day afield.

Let's say you're going pheasant hunting. It's early in the season, you're going to a place unfrequented by many other hunters, and it's a good guess the birds haven't been educated by being shot over too many times. You therefore anticipate taking shots at medium range—30 to 40 yards, let's say. A load of No. 6 or 5 through an Improved or Light Modified choke should do the trick, so let's shoot a couple of those loads at some paper and see what they're really doing at the pheasant end of things.

1. Staple a 40-inch square piece of paper with a 30-inch circle inked on it, or the NRA ST-2 Official Shotgun Patterning Target, to a backstop on your firearms range 40 yards distant from the firing line. Specific game animal targets, such as those for turkey, deer, ducks, and predators can also be used to perfect loads.

2. Choose a load and choke and make a note of it on a corner of the target.

3. Load up, shoulder your shotgun, aim at the center if the target, and quickly fire a round. Shouldering, aiming, and firing should be done in fairly rapid succession. This is not a long, deliberate aim as you would perform when shooting a rifle from the bench.

4. Unload, make sure the firing line has gone cold if you're shooting with other people (everyone has unloaded and put down their firearms) and retrieve your target.

5. Replace the target and repeat the procedure for each load and choke you anticipate using.

With several shot targets in hand, one for each choke and load combination, what do you see? Are the pellet hits evenly distributed or does it look like many of them clustered in one area? If they are clustered, was it in the kill zone area of the game you intend to hunt or does it look like it would produce a miss or, worse, a bad wounding shot on the animal? Do you have too few pellets in the center of the target and too many on the fringes? Is the overall pattern high or low, left or right on the target?

In our example of pheasants at 35 yards, you'd probably like a fairly even distribution of pellets on the target at 40 yards. You're shooting a moving object, and you should see enough pellets to understand that at least a couple or several are very likely to connect with the head for a fast kill, with just a few striking the body; you'll have to pick out some pellets when you clean the bird for dinner, but you would expect nearly all the meat to be edible. If you found your pattern was "tight," with a cluster of pellets in one area versus an even distribution, you might want to re-pattern that load with a slightly more open choke or save that choke/load combination for later in the season when the birds are educated and wary and flushing further away. (See the sidebar on pattern percentages for more detail.)

Answering these questions and then changing loads and chokes to best accommodate the game you'll be pursuing and the anticipated field conditions are essential to understanding how your shotgun performs. It will instill confidence in you as the shooter and minimize the chances of making a shot that wounds or misses.

Pattern Percentages

As you've seen in this chapter, the choke or constriction of the bore is an important consideration. Keeping the pattern tight or spread is equally important, given a good understanding of which is needed for the particular game.

There is no bull's-eye in shotgun testing. Choke effectiveness is gauged by firing at a target with a 30-inch circle at 40 yards. The percentages of shot inside this 30-inch circle for a given shot charge tells us how effective the choke tube is. For example, if there were the average 400 pellets in a 1-ounce No. 9 birdshot load and half that shot payload hit the target, then the pattern is 50 percent. Six of eight buckshot pellets (much larger than No. 9) would be a 75-percent pattern.

Small game at modest range needs an open choke. Larger game at longer range, such as ducks, requires a tighter choke. The chart below lists pellet count percentages you should see through today's commonly available chokes for shot payloads other than buckshot; yes, this means you'll have to actually take a marker and count the hits on your patterning target both within the 30-inch circle and outside it. (Buckshot follows its own rules; tight chokes sometimes work as designed with buckshot and sometimes not. You'll need to experiment to see what works best and throws the tightest, most consistent pattern.)

Choke	Pattern on a 30-inch Circle at 40 Yards
Super Full	Over 75 percent
Full	70 percent
Modified	60 percent
Improved Cylinder	50 percent
Open/Cylinder (no choke)	approximately 40 percent

Note: Open-choked riot guns are often marked "Open Cylinder." They sometimes fail to place even 30 percent of the charge on the target at 40 yards, which is why keeping them relegated to close-quarters work is a must. There are exceptions. My Benelli Nova tactical pump often patterns in the Improved Cylinder range at 40 yards, despite its Cylinder constriction. Bottom line, you won't know until you put it on paper.

Winchester's sporting loads represent millions of dollars of research into shot hardness, wads, and shot cups.

The Winchester PDX feature a combination of buckshot and a single slug.

Skeet and trap require excellent patterns and affordable shells.

Fiocchi offers first-class shells for every situation.

Now let's look at how pattering works for personal defense. The Cylinder bore common to most defensive shotguns throws an open pattern. This increases the chance of striking an attacker at close range; though "open" compared to other chokes, a Cylinder choke in a defensive shotgun is often more than tight enough inside of 15 yards to stop an aggressor.

With personal defense, it is important to keep the shotgun payload centered and to obtain a hit with the majority of it (usually buckshot). In some cases, a hit with half the buckshot payload may be effective, but it depends on the distance to your attacker, your choke, and where on their body the adversary is struck with the load.

Note: Sporting shotguns may be used in personal defense in an emergency, but they tend to be heavier than shotguns designed specifically for combat use. Sporting shotguns also have barrels of 22 to 34 inches in length, and this makes maneuvering them quickly in the home or other tight areas more difficult. For that reason, this book focuses on short-barreled shotguns for personal defense.

A combination of loads shows the versatility of the shotgun.

As I've said, shotguns are versatile tools, and, as such, come in a dizzying array of configurations. For 3-Gun competition, for instance, you want a shotgun that is comfortable to fire in long strings. A defensive shotgun, on the other hand, will be fired but a few times. Sporting shotguns have large recoil pads, and the self-loading action and stock designs of modern shotguns are intended to minimize recoil. A sporting shotgun will also feature an

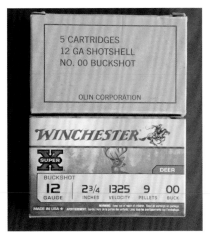

Winchester offers a variety of hard-hitting buckshot loads, including military standard.

aiming rib for use on moving game, while personal-defense guns usually lack this feature. An interchangeable choke tube system will allow the use of the shotgun for many types of purposes, and changing out a barrel from a longer one for skeet or duck hunting to a short, riot gun-type barrel instantly transforms the one

These buckshot shells are hard hitters.

shotgun and turns it into acceptable personal-defense shotgun.

Left to right, recovered from old books: 20-gauge buckshot, a Hornady slug, and a standard lead slug.

A sporting shotgun must handle quickly and largely by feel.

This Mossberg 500C 20-gauge is among the author's favorite recreational shotguns.

Still, while one shotgun can be made to accommodate many purposes, my recommendation is to use the field gun in the field and tailor the defensive shotgun to defense use. Otherwise, you will have a shotgun not well suited to either pursuit. (We will look at the different gauges in the next chapter.)

The author finds the light and lovely handling Mossberg 20-gauge a joy to fire.

CHAPTER 3

SHOTGUN GAUGES AND AMMUNITION PAIRINGS

Just as you need to look hard at the job you want to accomplish with the shotgun, you also need to think hard before choosing the gauge to be used for that job. While a blanket recommendation for the versatile and powerful 12-gauge is good for personal defense, the other gauges in some cases are appropriate and even superior for certain chores.

Hornady's SST and Superformance slug loads are high-tech.

WHAT IS A GAUGE?

Gauge as it relates to shotshell ammunition is an expression of a shotgun barrel bore dimension. Originally, gauge was determined first by using a solid lead ball that fits the bore perfectly, then expressing the weight of that single ball as a fraction of a pound. The number of balls that made up the pound then became the gauge. Today's 12-gauge is nominally .729-inch in bore size, thus, it would take 12 .729-inch balls weighing 1/12-pound each.

Gauges commonly available today are, from largest to smallest, 10-, 12-, 16-, 20-, and 28-gauge and .410-bore. (The .410 is actually a caliber designation, not a gauge). Gauges of eras past, mostly found in fowling pieces during the time of the market hunters, included 8-, 4-, and even 2-gauges. These last three are rare, but the truly obsolete shotgun bores include the 11-, 15-, 18-, and 3-gauges.

Shotguns may be named by gauge, but the bore diameter is useful to gauge power and the size relationship of one to the other:

1. 10-gauge = .780-inch
2. 12-gauge = .727-inch
3. 16-gauge = .670-inch
4. 20-gauge = .617-inch
5. 28-gauge = .550-inch
6. .410-bore = .410-inch

CHOOSING A GAUGE

Before choosing the gauge that is best for your use, you need to look at what a shotgun really does. The shotgun throws a pattern of numerous shot pellets that can strike and kill flying game, flying targets, static game and, as in the case of personal defense, a human attacker. The difference between the various gauges is in their power and performance.

For power, versatility, and availability, the best choice by far for any of these chores is the 12-gauge. It's also the most economical gauge. While it doesn't make sense at first that the larger and heavier 12-gauge would be the more affordable shell, the popularity of the gauge, its wide versatility in application, and the mass production of millions of shells make it so.

While Hornady isn't the oldest shotshell manufacturer, its developments are first-class.

Among the gauges smaller than the 12-gauge, the 20-gauge has much merit for all-around use for those wishing a lighter shotgun with generally less recoil. The 16-gauge (in between the 12- and 20-gauge), comes and goes in popularity, and the 28-gauge is a favorite with more expert bird hunters and among skeet shooters competing with the quartet of 12-, 20-, 28-gauge and .410-bore. The 10-gauge continues to find favor with serious waterfowlers and turkey hunters. Some big-game hunters and those keeping a shotgun handy for bear protection also utilize this big gauge. However, the heavy recoil and weighty guns keep the user pool of this gauge small.

Another consideration when choosing a shotgun gauge is to think about how much practice you plan on doing. The weight of the shotgun affects recoil, and while a heavy 12-gauge may kick in a similar fash-

Winchester's humble .410 slug is a credible performer for personal defense.

ion to a light 20-gauge, a light 12-gauge shotgun will typically kick harder with heavy loads. Shotguns are not generally aimed as rifles are (more on that in later chapters), but rather shot to connect with the target by feel. Sights can be important, but are far less so than with rifles. Regardless, if you are planning on hunting with a shotgun, get plenty of practice.

SHOT SIZES

Once you understand the differences in shotgun gauges, you need to look at the projectiles they throw. Some shot size, such as birdshot, is useful in all the gauges. Larger shot such as 00 Buckshot isn't as well suited to the small gauges. I'll cover slugs in the next chapter.

Shot sizes begin with the smallest Nos. 9, 8, 8½, and 7½ (in increasing size order, No. 9 being the smallest). These small pellets

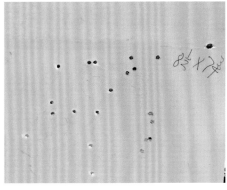

Whatever your pursuit, assessing the point of aim and point of impact and then measuring the pattern are important.

are used for bird hunting and clay bird competition. (The No. 8½ is used by some target shooters, but it's not as common as the other three). These small shot pellets break clay birds admirably and will also anchor a dove or quail without destroying the meat. For practice with defensive shotguns, these loads can also be ideal for young and smaller-statured shooters, as the recoil is light and the shotshells are affordable.

You may come across something called "rat shot" or "snake shot." This is very small No. 12 shot, and you'll most likely find it loaded in rifle or handgun ammunition for use against—you guessed it—rats and snakes and other small pests. These rather low-powered rounds are generally not considered suitable for personal defense.

Next up in size are Nos. 6, 5, and 4 (again, in increasing size order, with No. 6 being the smallest of the three). This gets the shotgun into the duck, pheasant, turkey, and rabbit range. Larger shot sizes, those running in increasing size order from Nos. 3, 2, 1, BB, BBB, T, and TT, generally find use with long-range waterfowlers, as do the less-common F (also known as TTT) and FF shot sizes. (These three biggest sizes—TT, F, and FF—are restricted in many locations).

For static game (e.g., deer) and predators, hunters will move into the various buckshot sizes. Buckshot starts with the smallest No. 4 Buck and progresses in size to Nos. 3, 2, 1, 0 (pronounced "single-ought"), 00 ("double-ought"), 00½ ("double-ought and a half"), 000 ("triple-ought"), 000½ ("triple-ought and a half"), and the largest 0000 ("four-ought") Buck.

Note: When it comes to personal defense, buckshot isn't overly effective in shotshells smaller than 20-gauge, and this combination should only be considered if the weight of the shotgun and recoil are overwhelming considerations for the user. In my opinion, the 12-gauge is best for personal defense based on its ability to stop an aggressor in the event deadly force is warranted, as well as the versatility of ammo choices available to the gauge.

Here are the actual pellet diameters for today's modern shot offerings:

1. No. 9 = .08-inch
2. No. 8½ = .085-inch
3. No. 8 = .09-inch
4. No. 7½ = .095-inch
5. No. 6 = .11-inch
6. No. 5 = .12-inch
7. No. 4 = .13-inch
8. No. 2 = .15-inch
9. No. 1 = .16-inch
10. BB = .18-inch
11. BBB = .19-inch

12. T = .20-inch
13. TT = .21-inch
14. F (or TTT) = .22-inch
15. FF = .23-inch
16. No. 4 Buck = .24-inch
17. No. 3 Buck = .25-inch
18. No. 2 Buck = .27-inch
19. No. 1 Buck = .30-inch
20. 0 Buck = .32-inch
21. 00 Buck = .33-inch
22. 00½ Buck = .34-inch
23. 000 Buck = .36-inch
24. 000½ Buck = .37-inch
25. 0000 Buck = .38-inch

SHOTSHELL SIZES WITHIN GAUGES

Shotshells within gauges come in different lengths. Over time, increasingly longer and more powerful shells have been introduced. For instance, in the 12-gauge, the 2¾-inch shell is the most common, but it is also available in 3-inch and 3½-inch configurations. (Specialty 2- and 2½-inch versions are very uncommon but can be ordered for the few shotguns chambered for them, usually side-by-sides of vintage production.)

Here's where shell length and user safety meet. A shotgun chambered for a shell size longer than 2¾-inch will accept and generally function with the shells shorter than its stated chambering. Thus, a shotgun chambered to take 3½-inch shells will accommodate 3- and 2¾-inch shells. A 3-inch chambered shotgun will also take 2¾-inch shells. The converse is *not* true. You should *never* attempt to chamber a round in a shotgun that is bigger than the chambering stamped on the barrel or receiver. Gauges are another facet of

A 28-inch-barreled semi-automatic shotgun such as the Remington 1100 is ideal for many sporting uses.

shotgunning that are not inter-changeable. *Never* load a shotgun shell that into a gun that's marked for another gauge.

The ability of some shotguns to chamber a variety of shell lengths is what makes them so appealing: One tool can be made to work well in a variety of applications. My personal Benelli Nova shotgun, for instance, has never been fired with anything save 2¾-inch shell, but I like that the longer shells are an option if I need them.

Steel shot was a game changer for the waterfowl hunting industry. The major makers have all developed effective steel loads, as well as other advanced non-lead shot designs.

The 2¾-, 3-, and 3½-inch shells give the 12-gauge shotgun great versatility.

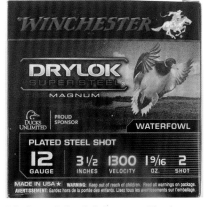

Winchester's Dry Lok Supersteel loads are impressive performers.

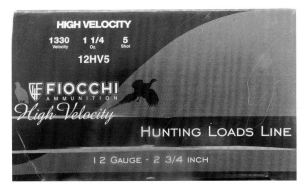

Fiocchi offers a good line of shells with excellent performance.

SHOT MAKEUP—LEAD VS. STEEL

Lead has been the primary choice for shot pellet construction since its inception in the late 1700s. Why lead? It's a metal that is dense and easily formed into a useful projectile. Today, some shot has a copper coating, for when harder shot is desired, such as for hunting deer-sized game. This helps ensure that penetration is adequate and will reach a vital organ for a quick and humane kill. When using buckshot for personal defense and or for predator hunting, it is more desirable that the balls are soft and even deform to an extent, in order to create larger wound channels and to prevent over-penetration.

Non-lead shot was mandated for all waterfowl hunting nationwide beginning in 1991. Due to that new regulation, and to meet the demand imposed by other such lead shot restrictions on some state lands since then, ammunition makers first created steel shot. A number of other non-lead alternatives have been offered in the ensuing years, including shot made of bismuth, a tungsten/iron combination, and others.

This is a birdshot pattern at moderate range.

Steel was thought to be an ideal alternative to lead, as it was harder. However, its killing power in the earliest days of the lead ban was criticized; many waterfowlers expressed their frustration with poor patterning, poor kills, and wounded birds. Steel also couldn't be used in many older guns without causing barrel damage, and the Full choke favored by many waterfowlers

A No. 5 shot pattern, useful for ducks.

Buckshot is offered in several sizes. The 00 and 000 sizes are popular choices, each delivering powerful and effective loads. Patterning your shotgun will tell the story of which load you should use.

Nine 00 Buck pellets at 1,300 feet per second (fps) is an industry standard for performance. This is Winchester's newest offering for 3-Gun competition.

accustomed to shooting lead weren't safe to use with steel. The industry answered with much-improved steel shot loads, including the wad inside the shells that helped improve patterning and better protect barrels. New shotguns were produced that better handled hard steel shot, as were new choke tubes that tightened up patterns without increasing pressures at the muzzle and damaging

You must pattern the shotgun and be certain you know the effective range of buckshot.

barrels. Hard, dense shot made of other non-lead metals also made their appearance.

There are many great-performing non-lead shotshells on the market today, and whether you decide to use them by choice or are required to because of where you hunt, there are a couple things to bear in mind. The first is that steel shot must never be used in an older, fixed Full-choke shotguns. In a modern shotgun with screw-in chokes, the Full choke tube must also be marked for use with steel shot to be safe.

Most if not all boxed commercial shotgun loads will be marked with the weight of the shot payload. Common payloads you'll see on store shelves include: ½-oz. (.410-bore) ¾-oz. (28-gauge), ⅞-oz. (commonly 20- and 12-gauge), 1 oz. (20-gauge through 120-gauge), 1⅛-oz. (12-gauge), 1½-oz.

Shotgun shells and their boxes are clearly marked for shot size and sometimes pellet material.

(12- and 10-gauge), and 2-oz. (10-gauge). Keep in mind the earlier discussion about shell length within a gauge. This means that a 12-gauge 3-inch shell holds more powder and shot than a 2¾-inch shell, and a 3½-inch shell holds even more.

PUTTING IT ALL TOGETHER

The shotgun for personal defense is best regarded as part of a tactical "system." This is in respect to the great versatility of the shotgun and its payloads. The shotgun may be used in fast-moving, short-range tactical scenarios. It may be fired in the home with devastating effect upon an invader, but, with the right choice of ammunition, have little chance of injury to a neighbor. The shotgun may also be loaded with slugs that may be effective well past 100 yards or a tightly patterning load of pellets that do a great job of stopping an aggressor at short range. It all hinges upon choosing the proper load, understanding how that load performs with your gun, and being skilled enough to make the shot count when you need it.

For qualified users, the shotgun may also be used with distraction devices, door-breaching loads, or even paint marker loads. Shotguns are used with special munitions to scare birds from the runways of major airports and kept handy on fishing boats in order to put down thrashing, dangerous sharks brought up with a catch.

The loads discussed in the following pages are well-suited to tactical shotgun use. I tested each in both pump-action and self-loading shotguns. Let's look at some of the various types of loads available.

Practice Loads

Quality loads using birdshot—small, light shot intended for hunting flying game birds in those Nos. 7½, 8, and 9 sizes—are ideal for practice. There is little recoil in most loads up to the 2 ¾-inch 12-gauge 1¼-ounce load. At short, personal-defense range, they will pattern similarly to buckshot, just with hundreds of holes rather than the few from a buckshot load.

I do not support the idea that birdshot makes a suitable self-defense load. In my testing, birdshot has proven capable of penetrating four to six inches of simulated tissue. I feel this is inadequate for personal defense, particularly if the assailant is heavily clothed.

If you must use a lighter shot load for home defense, then Nos. 4 or 6 or a heavy turkey load are indicated. These loads can also be enjoyable for shorter practice sessions and offer some monetary savings over buckshot and slug loads.

All that said, be certain to get practice time in with buckshot, even if you spend the majority of your practice time with light loads. You have to know where those eight or nine pellets of 00 Buckshot in a 12-gauge 2¾-inch load will be flying at various distances. For instance, at seven yards, my old open choke Remington 870 will deliver eight 00 pellets from Hornady's Critical Defense load into a pattern approximately 5.5x6 inches. This is ideal for personal defense. However, as the range increases to 20 yards, that same load through that same gun no longer places the majority of the pellets on a man-sized target. In between, I found that 15 yards is the outermost range for effectiveness with this gun and buckshot combination. Your gun and ammo combination could pattern differently, but that is why patterning is so important.

Buckshot

Twelve-gauge buckshot comes in several shell lengths and power levels, including 2¾-inch, 3-inch, and 3½-inch sizes. The 2¾-inch shells are plenty strong for personal defense and generate all of the recoil you likely to wish to endure.

The most common buckshot sizes are 000, 00, and No. 4 Buck. While each has merit in certain situations, the preponderance of evidence in my testing points to the effectiveness of the 00 Buckshot loading. One exception to this I've come to favor has been Hornady's No. 4 Varmint Express.

Originally intended for use against predators such as coyotes at the limits of ethical shotgun hunting ranges, this load uses 24 No. 4 Buck pellets and patterns *very* tightly at personal-defense ranges.

There are two general types of modern buckshot loads, standard-velocity and reduced-recoil loads. The reduced-recoil loads were developed for police using pump-action riot guns. These shotguns are shorter and lighter than sporting guns and can produce painful recoil with full-power buckshot load. Reducing the shot payload velocity from 1,300 to 1,200 fps results in much greater comfort and control. Even better, the

These lower-powered loads were delivered at 10 yards, the head shot at seven yards with Federal's Personal Defense 00 Buckshot.

patterns with reduced-recoil buckshot are tighter than with full-power loads out of these short, light shotguns.

Among the leaders in the reduced-recoil field has been Federal Cartridge. Its Personal Defense shotshell with Federal's proprietary Flitecontrol wad is a reduced-recoil load that has given excellent results in testing and in use by police agencies. Powerful and controllable at the same time, this is a first-class personal-defense loading. Hornady's Critical Defense eight-pellet 00 12-gauge load is another reduced-recoil load that makes for a tighter pattern. This load is useful in semi-automatic shotguns and is among the tightest-patterning 00 buckshot loads I've tested.

CHAPTER 4

SHOTGUN SLUGS

A slug is to a shotshell what a bullet is to a rifle or handgun cartridge: It is simply one solid projectile. Slug construction generally falls into two categories, full-bore and saboted.

FULL-BORE SLUGS

There are two names closely associated with full-bore slugs that you'll commonly see on boxes of slugs at your local retailer, Brenneke and Foster.

The Brenneke's were developed just before the turn of the twentieth century by Wilhelm Brenneke, a German firearms and ammunition maker. These slugs are usually of solid lead with slanted ribs on their sides, which aren't about spinning the projectile, as some think, but are instead there to stabilize irregularities in weight distribution throughout the slug that may have occurred in their casting. The ribs also decrease friction in smooth (non-rifled) bores, thereby boosting velocity, and they take the deformation imparted by the squeeze through the choke, rather than compromising the slug itself. Most Brenneke slugs are solid lead.

Foster slugs appeared several decades after Brenneke's. Their invention is pegged to Karl M. Foster's design work in 1931, though a patent for them wasn't completed until 1947. Designed specifically for smoothbore shotguns, Foster slugs are "weight-forward"—meaning they are cast to have the majority of their weight in the nose of the slug—and have a deep hollow at their rear. Think of them like you would a shuttlecock in the game of Badminton. Like the Brenneke's, most Foster slugs have ribs on their outside, and they are also mostly solid lead in their construction.

Weighing an ounce in 3-inch 12 gauge loads, slugs of the older, soft-lead Foster type slugs are legendary stoppers at closer ranges (usually under 75 yards); the standard 2¾ inch 12-gauge shell uses a 7/8-ounce slug and are also excellent at reduced ranges. While not as accurate as a sabot slug through a rifled shotgun barrel, Foster and Brenneke slugs have their advantage in their slug's solid lead construction. This soft lead tends to expand upon impact (i.e., creates a bigger hole), and even break off pieces, which create additional wound channels and damage. Their drawback lies in their reduced penetration compared to saboted slugs, which is why they are best left to reduced-range applications and select targets. Very large animals such as the big bears are not the best targets for these soft lead slugs.

Foster and Brenneke slugs are soft because the maker cannot control what type of shotgun or choke the slug will be fired in. A hard lead slug or one made of materials harder than lead traveling through a super-tight choke would be squeezed as it exited the barrel, but it wouldn't compress like soft lead would, and this would generate a spike in pressure, perhaps even destroying the gun and injuring its shooter. Thus, Brenneke and Foster slugs are made soft enough to deform as they travel through the barrel and whatever choke might be present at the end.

I have fired four-inch 50-yard groups with my smoothbore Cylinder-choked Remington 870 and these old-style slugs. Some will do a little better than this, but this is plenty accurate for hunting medium-sized game to 50 yards or a little beyond. The Foster slug is easily swaged down by the tightest choke and, as a rule, they are safer to use than very hard slugs with a tight choke. (Accuracy often suffers when any slug is fired in a Full-choke shotgun.) Foster slugs will sometimes badly foul a rifled barrel with their lead, so while you can fire a Foster or Brenneke slug in a rifled shotgun barrel, that shouldn't be your first choice.

You may encounter slugs marked as "reduced recoil." While it's true that the slugs you might want to employ for self-defense work or game-getting can have considerable recoil, I don't think their reduced-recoil options (unlike reduced-recoil buckshot which I do sometimes recommend), are something you should consider without significant time on the bench working with them. The reduced-recoil slug drops significantly at long range due to its reduced velocity. At the same time, it actually penetrates *more* than the full-power slug due to reduced expansion. In the end, the full-power slug offers greater wound potential and greater range.

SABOTED SLUGS

A counterpoint to the old soft lead slug is the modern hard lead or steel slug that rides inside a sabot. Saboted slugs are intended for use in rifled shotgun barrels, those barrels having a cut groove within them that turns through the barrel's length—just like a rifle or handgun barrel. Saboted slugs wear a wad similar to that found in shot and buckshot shells. The wad is gripped by the rifling as it and its slug travel down the barrel, imparting spin and velocity, just as it would a rifle or handgun bullet. Because the slug never has physical contact with the barrel, saboted slugs can be constructed with metals harder than lead, such as steel, copper, and even brass.

You can fire a saboted slug in a smoothbore shotgun, but accuracy with this combo will suffer. Also, it isn't unusual for saboted slugs to keyhole—turn on their sides during flight—and strike the target sideways when fired from smooth shotgun bores, and that essentially ruins penetration and expansion.

Of the three slug designs, saboted slugs are generally regarded as being the most accurate and capable of big-game kills at distances in the 100-plus yard range, and hunters employing a rifled barrel with saboted slugs for hunting will likely also mount a scope or at least rifle sights on their shotguns for accurate shots at such distances.

Saboted slugs are undersized—less than bore or gauge size—in order to promote safety even in a tight choke. The sabot also seals with the bore as it travels, improving velocity. Saboted slugs typically weigh the same as shot columns, 7/8- or 1-ounce, sometimes heavier. Recoil can be substantial with these loads.

Today, most folks using slugs in their shotguns do so because centerfire rifles are disallowed in their hunting area. Of course, there are those who also simply appreciate their deadly performance. They understand how hard a shotgun hits at close range and find the slug a great deer- and boar-stopper. This can be important if you're in an emergency situation in which protein sources are scarce, and that also makes slugs a viable option when it comes to self-defense.

You need to know that if you choose to go with a rifled shotgun barrel and saboted slugs, that firearm will be dedicated to that purpose, i.e., it will not be a multi-purpose firearm,

Two shotgun loads delivered in a fast manner produced this pattern.

as firing shotshells down a rifled barrel is not recommended and doing so does not provide the performance that firing those same shotshells down a smoothbore will.

I have experimented with slugs for more than thirty years. None are more effective than Lightfield slugs. Lightfield offers a wide variety of slugs, from those that have little recoil to those that are guaranteed to produce the most energy and knockdown power in their class. For instance, the Lightfield Hybred Lite load sends a 1¼-ounce slug at just 1,300 fps versus the usual 1,600 fps. This is a good load for those using lighter shotguns (there will be less recoil than with the full-power load), and for personal defense.

Lightfield's highly developed slugs set many power and accuracy standards.

The Lightfield Hybred slug was an outstanding performer in the author's testing.

The 1¼-ounce Hybred Express slug exits a 20-inch barrel at an impressive 1,450 fps. Lightfield says that at a long 150 yards, this slug retains roughly 1,120 ft-lbs of energy—that is impressive! There is also a 3-inch shell available with the Hybred slug, the Hybred Elite. This one broke around 1,700 fps from the TriStar Tec12 self-loader in which I tested it. I

Note that the Lightfield slug is rated for medium to large game.

am unaware of a load with greater punch than this Lightfield Hybred. It is similar to hitting a deer-sized game animal with an elephant rifle—well, not quite, but you get the point. The big slug simply does the business.

If you have a shotgun with a rifled barrel and can perfect your marksmanship skills, the Hybred slugs are accurate well past 100 yards, even 150 with the proper equipment.

The thing to remember with slugs is that you'll need to deliberately aim the shotgun as you would a rifle to ensure an accurate connection with your target and for the impact to have its intended effect. This means you'll have to sight-in your shotgun and slug combination, just as you would a rifle and rifle cartridge combination.

To test accuracy thoroughly requires a serious dedication to your

Old dry text books versus Lightfield slugs.

grip on the gun, a solid bench rest, and a good recoil pad. Any miss and deviation from the zero inside of 100 yards are likely related to shooter error more so than the accuracy of the slug or the shotgun. Keep the shotgun steady, lean into the butt, and keep the support hand pressing the shotgun to the rear and into your shoulder. Gain the proper sight picture and squeeze the trigger.

In my experience, you do not need a rifled slug bore shotgun to use the Lightfield slugs well. The sabot type slug combination actually expands in the bore as a result of back pressure on firing. The sabot slug locked to the barrel and gives good accuracy. A rifled slug barrel will give the finest accuracy, but an open Cylinder barrel will give excellent results to 50 yards and a bit beyond, making the Lightfield slug an excellent option for hunting in dense cover, as well as an option for those who do not wish to equip their shotgun with a rifled barrel.

The saboted slugs intended for long range use such as the Hornady SST slugs are capable of excellent accuracy to even 200 yards. Some claim even greater accuracy, but that generally requires a shotgun specifically designed for slug accuracy.

The 20-gauge Hornady SST I tested sends a 250-grain projectile at 1,800 fps. This means that a shooter with this load is getting *monster* .454 Casull handgun performance! From my short-barreled coach gun, the load actually breaks over 1,600 fps, and that's good; a 28-inch sporting gun would coax the full velocity and accuracy from this load. The 12-gauge saboted Hornady SST sends a 300-grain bullet at 2,000 fps. In my testing at personal-defense distances, the SST slugs struck to the point of aim in the 12-gauge and a bit low in the 20-gauge. Either way, they're both excellent rounds when fired through rifled barrels.

SIGHTING IN SLUGS FOR TACTICAL APPLICATIONS

To sight the shotgun with slugs for tactical applications, I begin by standing seven yards from my sighting target. If you're familiar with sighting in a rifle, then you also know that most of that work is done while seated at a bench and almost never at such a short distance. I'll emphasize that I choose to stand when looking for *combat* zero, because I want to know what it's doing when I'm shooting it as I would in a self-defense scenario.

I place the bead on the center of the target and fire. I check the hit to see if it is high or low and check radial dispersion. Of course, with a bead-sighted shotgun, there's no rear sight to raise or lower and change the point of impact. But it is possible to change the way you hold the shotgun and where you hold your point of aim to effect the impact point you desire. For instance, if the head is held high and off of the shotgun, the shotgun may shoot high (and you'll likely get a nice bruise on your jaw or cheekbone).

Confirm your combat zeroing work at five, 10, and 15 yards, in addition to your initial seven-yard work, then move to 25 yards once you're controlling your hits well at the 15. Depending on your shotgun and its accuracy, you may want to work your way out to 50 yards or more. Just remember that, at these greater distances, your shooting skills will need to be solid and your aiming sure and deliberate to connect. If you're looking for speedy hits way out there, you'll need to start slowly and build those skills.

If your shotgun is your only firearm and you intend to use both slugs and shot, be certain you know where each of your loads strikes in relation to the point of aim. For instance, drills in which you fire a load of buckshot at a 10-yard target followed by a slug fired at 25 or 35 yards, and also at targets set at the same distance, will quickly tell you how you'll have to adjust your hold on the shotgun and its aim to make accurate hits with either load.

LONG-DISTANCE SLUG WORK

Even with a smoothbore riot gun, slugs may give the shooter surprising accuracy to 50 yards. My Benelli pump-action riot gun, for instance, will hold four Lightfield slugs into 3½ inches at 50 yards if I do my part. (Part of the advantage of the Benelli over other types of riot guns is that the Benelli is supplied with ghost ring sights, and that's something you might consider accessorizing your shotgun with if you intend to keep it mostly for slug work.)

Many currently produced rifled-barrel slug guns are plenty accurate for deer-sized game to 150 yards. That may benefit you if you need to put food on the table, but my primary goal in utilizing slugs is to penetrate light cover and to take out an adversary past buckshot range. For the active shooter behind cover, slugs will do the business if the shooter does their part.

It's at distance work that you can also consider the shotgun for substitute rifle shooting. Just know that your trigger control becomes much more important as you address targets past 25 yards. The trigger is pressed straight to the rear. There is no jerking or milking the trigger to one side or the other. Do not rush. Press the trigger smoothly and steadily until the trigger breaks.

Long-distance work should initially be done from the bench, just as you would when firing with a rifle. However, the shotgun's recoil is different than a rifle's, and if you do not hold the shotgun correctly, you will find that your slugs will be all over the target. To accomplish a high level of accuracy takes a bit of an unusual hold described by the slug maker Lightfield in this manner:

Position a solid rest under both the fore-end and butt portions of your gun's stock. Begin applying shoulder pressure to the butt of the gun and offset any forward gun movement by pulling straight back with your right hand in trigger squeezing position. With your left hand on the fore-end, pull firmly straight back and down at a 45-degree angle. The firmer the hold, the better the accuracy will be. Keep in mind that 60 percent of your overall group size can be directly attributed to inconsistent hand pressure. If the tips of your fingers are not turning white and/or the gun tends to fly out of your hands, your hold is weak and so too will be your groups.

Although rifled slug guns perform similarly to rifles, they are not rifles and cannot be zeroed as if they were. Even the fastest slug has a significantly longer barrel time than a typical rifle bullet. It is extremely important to apply the same back pressure to the fore-end and the buttstock in the field as is done at the range! Not doing so will result in the barrel jumping into the air, moving your point of aim, and ruining your shot before the slug even exits the barrel.

Sighting in slugs for distance should start at 50 yards, not 100. A good measure of accuracy for most 2¾-inch shells is to have them sighted in to strike 2.5 inches high at 50 yards, for then gravity will have it dead on at 100.

Lightfield Slugs for Accuracy

The Lightfield slug eliminates some of the inaccuracy associated with bore size variations within a gauge. When fired, the pressure build-up behind the Lightfield projectile forces the slug and sabot assembly to expand to the actual full bore size of *all* shotgun barrels, regardless the barrel manufacturer. Once expanded, the locked sabot and slug assembly takes full advantage of the barrel rifling, maximizes spin, and ensures an incredibly accurate flight path. In essence, the round becomes "customized" to whatever gun you have.

FULL-POWER VERSUS REDUCED-RECOIL SLUGS

For the majority of personal defense needs, I prefer to use reduced-recoil buckshot. However, a shotgun slug, in my experience, is more likely to produce an immediate cessation of hostilities than a load of buckshot.

Like buckshot, slugs come in full-power and reduced-recoil loadings. The reduced-recoil slug is a good alternative for those who can't handle the thump of the full-power slugs. Their modest loss in velocity means little at combat ranges, but they do drop significantly at longer ranges. Take time to consider this and practice at different distances with these loads so you know what to expect and where to aim as distance dictates.

A proper point of aim results in center hits.

Full-power and even magnum loads should be your choice if the likely threat is a large or dangerous animal. This means mastering heavier recoil. To keep yourself in the game, keep sessions at the range short, taking frequent breaks and shooting shorter strings than you would with lighter loads.

At some point, a shotgun utilized with slug loads must be properly sighted from a benchrest firing position.

TOP SLUG LOADS FOR THE TACTICAL SHOTGUN

Slug loads are indicated when there is a need for either great penetration or great precision. A load that splits the difference is the Winchester PDX1 12-gauge. This load is housed in a distinctive black hull. The payload is three 00 pellets riding on top of a 1-ounce rifled slug. The design promotes buckshot hits at close range, while also providing coverage at long range with the slug, all within one load.

The all-steel DDupleks slug is an impressive performer.

This is an interesting option. In the past, many law enforcement officers kept a mix of loads in the shotgun, usually two buckshot loads followed by two slugs. With the PDX1 load you have buck and ball in one load.

Another favorite of mine is Federal Cartridge's TruBall slugs, which were designed to give optimum accuracy even in smoothbore shotguns. It offers deep penetration and extreme shock, due to its size and velocity.

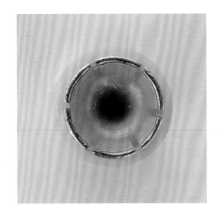

When defense against large animals is a consideration, this slug would be a wise choice.

While the old round-nose lead slug is still effective, there have been improvements in slug design that increase wound potential and accuracy while also limiting ricochet. Century International Arms offers the DDupleks 12-gauge steel and polyethylene slug loads is one of those improvements. These slugs are imported from Latvia. They are readily available, affordable, and offered in different configurations. The Monolit 28, for example, features an aerodynamically designed slug of steel with a polymer sheath to allow use in a steel barrel. The slug weights 435 grains and has an advertised muzzle velocity of 1,460 fps. I only consider actual damage as a measure of cartridge effectiveness, but this load develops a solid 1,963 ft-lbs of energy, which indicates it should be very effective on target.

I fired the slug for accuracy in my old standby rifle-sighted Remington 870. At 15 yards, three slugs were touching on the paper. At a long 50 yards, I fired a three-shot group of four inches. I'll take that.

To test wound potential with this slug, I used water jugs. These are six inches wide and offer a reasonable correlation to ballistic gelatin testing. The Steelhead Monolit 28, a 440-grain slug, penetrated seven water jugs and bounced into the eighth, *demonstrating 42 inches of penetration.* The design of the slug is intended to limit ricochet. The Monolit 28 slug is both accurate and powerful enough to be used in addressing dangerous animals and engaging adversaries behind cover. The similar Monolit 32 uses a larger 495-grain slug at 1,357 fps. This slug generated the greatest recoil of any of the loads tested. Penetration was less than with the Monolit 28 at just 36 inches of water and there was no deformation of the projectile. Accuracy is

These are impressive slugs!

The Latvian-produced DDupleks slugs gave fine results in all testing.

comparable to the Monolit 28. The comparison tells the tale. The Monolit 32 is a heavyweight loading with more smash at short-range than the smaller projectile, but with less overall penetration.

The most interesting and potentially effective load for personal defense I found in my testing for this book is the Hexolit 32. Another in the DDupleks lineup, this slug is designed to offer greatly improved wound potential and limit ricochet. The 495-grain Hexolit slug is similar to the others in its weight class, but this is an expanding slug that has the additional component of a ring of six shard-like projectiles sheathed in a polymer housing.

Average velocity for the 12-gauge Hexolit is 1,472 fps. Accuracy during my testing was good, but not on the level of the other loads; I shot a three-shot 50-yard group of about five inches. Yet I see this as acceptable, since the Hexolit is intended to be used at moderate range.

When fired into water, the Hexolit slug demonstrates nose section loss. DDupleks claims that the six metal pieces of the nose will be thrown away from the main slug in a radial pattern upon a hard impact, or expand away from the nose in other situa-

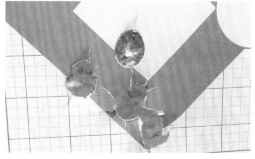

tions. Per my testing, the nose of the slug shed the petals as designed. In my first test-firing, there were holes in the second and third water jugs from the petals, but only one petal was actually found *in* the water jugs. This confirms radial dispersion.

This is good accuracy for a standard riot shotgun barrel.

Average penetration was 24 inches, much less than other slugs. The tradeoff is that the Hexolit demonstrates *impressive* wounding. Either through the shedding of its shard-like fingers or expansion with them intact, these projectiles creating a bigger and more jagged wound channel. Damage to my water jugs was visibly more than with the solid slugs. Coupled with its accuracy, this slug is an excellent option, in my opinion, for personal-defense use. Ricochet potential is difficult to gauge, but the slug should be less offensive than standard round-nose type slugs.

I found a third DDupleks slug, the Dupo 28, another interesting option. Similar to the Hexolit, this slug expands to well over an inch; my recovered slugs, demonstrated 1.1- to 1.4-inch diameters. For defense against feral dogs, this is a great option, and the heavy slugs would be a preferred choice for defense against bears.

Finally, of the great performers I have tested and found effective, accurate, and performing as advertised, perhaps my top pick is the Hornady Superformance slug. They are innovative in design for a slug and have a reputation for deep penetration. At the slug's heart—or its tip, if you will—is Hornady's famed MonoFlex Flex Tip. This tip was originally designed for use in lever-action cartridges. Lever-action cartridges have traditionally been round-nosed so that, in their tubular magazine, one does not set off a chain firing reaction when the bullet tip from one round contacts the primer of the round in front of it during recoil. The MonoFlex had the added benefit of providing deep penetration, something often absent in a round-nose rifle bullet design. Added to Hornady's bullet-shaped, copper-zinc alloy (95 percent copper) slug in an internal sabot, shooters get a slug that penetrates deeply and expands reliably, even at long range and low impact velocities.

The MonoFlex is available in both 12- and 20-gauge. As a change, I did most of my testing work for this round in the 20-gauge. I found the Mono-Flex accurate in my Mossberg 20-gauge pump, a smoothbore, and even though Hornady recommends this slug be used in a rifled barrel, at 20 yards the slug was quite accurate. This may not happen in other shotguns, it is simply my observation, but I'd certainly say that, if a 20-gauge is your choice for a personal-defense or hunting shotgun, this slug is well worth your time on the bench.

CHAPTER 5

SHOTGUN GAUGE APPLICATIONS FOR EMERGENCY PREPAREDNESS

Now that you know a bit about the various shotgun gauges and their ammunition, it's time to look at how it all works together. Seeking to find optimum gauge and load combinations that would be suitable for everything from the defense of food stores from four-legged predators to those that defend human life, I and a group of experienced friends headed to the range. Following are the results of our time afield.

THE .410-BORE

When it comes to the .410-bore shotgun shell, I found the majority of shooters in my test group had little use for it, with one even referring to it as "useless." One did insist that the .410 with slugs is a great predator gun and kills better than any .22-caliber rifle. I mention this before getting into the test results, because most of us involved with the testing came to a different opinion of the .410 by the time we were finished.

The .410 shotgun has enjoyed a new range of development in recent years, due to the introduction of a revolver that fires the .410 shotgun cartridge. That gun, the Taurus Judge, chambers both a .45 Colt handgun/rifle cartridge and .410-bore shotshell. Safety note: *Never* chamber a .45 Colt rifle/handgun cartridge in a .410-bore shotgun.

Winchester's slim .410 features a long shot column.

Despite that firearm's popularity with the home-defense crowd, this is a book about shotguns, so I'll keep the focus there.

A .410-bore shotgun is always an interesting firearm, and the one we used for this book's testing purpose was a Mossberg 500 pump-action with a 24-inch barrel. Hardly a "tactical" model, this shotgun features a gold trigger, vent rib, and smooth action. Overall, it's a very neat and fast-handling shotgun. Everyone enjoyed handling this shotgun during testing.

Despite a tight pattern, there is often a pellet off to one side or the other at ranges past 10 yards.

I began testing with birdshot to gauge the effect of it for personal defense. Next, several buckshot loads, including those specifically designed for personal defense, were given a run. Finally came the .410 slug. Loads were tested for patterns at seven yards and for penetration in water jugs at 10 feet or less. Here's what we tested:

Estate Cartridge High Velocity Hunting Load

This is a 3-inch shell, rated at high velocity, loaded with No. 6 shot. This load burned clean and offered a decent pattern for small-game hunting. At 10 feet, the swarm of birdshot penetrated only about seven inches of water

As range increases, so does the size of the pattern. The large holes are torn by the spent wad following the shot payload.

despite a velocity of some 1,170 feet per second (fps). The first group of pellets settled into the bottom of the first jug, and the ones that penetrated the second jug settled to the bottom just inside the jug. A half-dozen or so may have made a dent in the back of the second jug.

My opinion here: Birdshot should not be used for personal defense in any shotgun caliber if buckshot is available and can be trained with. I judge the penetration of birdshot to be inadequate. There is a substantial chance the shot would be stopped by a heavy leather jacket or other heavy clothing, not to mention fat and muscle.

Federal Premium .410 Handgun

With four 000 Buck balls as the payload in this 2½-inch shell, this is a heavier load than other .410 shells of this size. Recoil was light, as expected. This load gave an excellent pattern, measuring 2.75 by 2.5 inches at seven yards. Powder burn was clean. The buckshot reached 35 inches in water with no deflection. This is more than enough for personal defense, perhaps even a bit much, as is true of almost all buckshot loads—but then, buckshot was meant to take down a deer.

I was actually surprised by the penetration this load exhibited. Compared to a 12-gauge 000 load, this .410 load has less of a shot payload but displayed equal penetration.

Golden Bear Buckshot

When traveling to the gunshop and rounding up loads for this test, I spotted the Golden Bear brand and picked these up as a lark. These shells contain five No. 4 Buck pellets. What looked like a brass-cased shotgun shell is actually brass-plated steel. The load is pretty light as No. 4 Buck is far lighter than 000 Buck pellets, which weigh about 70 grains each; No. 4 Buck pellets come in at 20 grains. Velocity was good at some 1,370 fps, and the pattern was excellent at 3.5 inches high and two inches wide. There was no problem with feeding reliability in the Mossberg. Penetration was over 20 inches in water, but the energy is about half of the heavier loads. Because of the latter, I wouldn't recommend this as a defense load, but it would have merit for short-range pests.

Winchester PDX1 .410 Defender

This is a load I tested with great expectations. More expensive than the other loads, the PDX1 contains an interesting duplex payload: There are 12 plated BB-sized pellets and three .410 Cylinder-diameter plated discs in this 2½-inch shell. I sacrificed one shell, cutting it open to weigh the payload and calculate energy. The total payload is over 300 grains.

With this duplex load design, the PDX1 is intended to give a swarm of pellets at close range while also offering these solid projectiles for added penetration and effect at longer range. The result is the largest pattern at seven yards, seven by three inches. The flat disks grouped into about three inches, the rest taken up with the 12 BB pellets.

I feel we have penetration in the ideal range for personal defense without risking over-penetration with the PDX1 Defender. The greatest distance traveled by a single BB pellet was 24 inches in water. The slugs went 18 inches. This is good performance, with a good payload and pattern, and I view it as a true personal-defense load rather than a hunting or pest-control load.

Winchester Super X 413RS5

This is a ¼-ounce 3-inch rifled slug load. This is a traditional .410 slug that has proven suitable accurate in quite a few shotguns. Recoil was light and accuracy was much greater than expected. The ¼-ounce (about 109 grains, .392-caliber or so) slug went into the same hole at 15 yards for three rounds, impressive. Even firing offhand and using a bead front sight, seldom did I fire more than a one-inch three-shot group at 15 yards. Ballistic media testing was equally impressive. The slug penetrated 12 inches in water, making a dent in the outer cover of the third water jug. The slug upset well and retained 103 grains when weighed.

I have to agree with the opinion of one of the raters, Boyd, about this slug and gun combination. Boyd is a farmer and recognizes that the .410 is light and handy and doesn't take up much space. It is a killer on feral dogs and fox, and though it doesn't, of course, cover distance like a rifle, it can offer surprising accuracy. This slug is definitely an option in the .410. At 1,955 fps, the Winchester slugs we tested were more than 150 fps faster than Winchester claims. I think penetration would still be on the light side against a heavily bundled felon, but from what we saw, this slug has merit.

I want to emphasize that the slug we tested has its merits as a home-defense round. Velocity and energy are excellent, more than I would have guessed before beginning the test program. The slug is the least likely of the loads tested to over-penetrate. This was unexpected by most of the raters. The slug performs well and shoots to the point of aim with excellent accuracy. It is an option that cannot be discounted.

In the end, the .410 shotgun seems useful for personal defense. The raters agree that a slightly built person or youth would be well-served with the .410 shotgun if they cannot handle a larger gauge. We all enjoyed shooting the .410 and found it would not be out of place as an all-around pest popper (useful when trying to guard precious food supplies) and personal-defense shotgun.

Test Results

Load	Shell Length	Velocity	Standard Deviation	Muzzle Energy	Penetration	Group/Pattern Accuracy at 7 Yards
WW 000	3-inch	1,130 fps	14	992 ft-lbs	36 inches	3 × 2 inches
WW 000	2½-inch	1,144 fps	19	610 ft-lbs	36 inches	3 × 3 inches
Golden Bear	3-inch	1,372 fps	34	417 ft-lbs	30 inches	3.5 × 2 inches
Winchester PDX1	2½-inch	1,171 fps	28	928 ft-lbs	24 inches (pellets); 18 inches (discs)	7 × 3 inches
Federal Premium .410 Handgun	2½-inch	1,205 fps	26	902 ft-lbs	35 inches	3 × 3.5 inches
Winchester Super X Slug	3-inch	1,955 fps	22	993 ft-lbs	12 inches	1 × 1 inch (at 15 yards)

Note: Retained weight is only applicable to the PDX1, as it was the only ammunition for which all of the payload was recovered. The slug was recovered with about 95% of its weight retained.

28-GAUGE

The 28-gauge is a neat little shell that started life as a 2½-inch shell with a 1¾ dram charge of blackpowder. Today the 28-gauge holds ¾-ounce of shot in a 2¾-inch shell and long ago switched its power source to modern smokeless powders. The 28-gauge is a light and lovely shotshell with many uses, but, in my opinion, it is the least-versatile shotgun gauge and much too light for large game.

These are 28-gauge shells compared to a single 12-gauge. The 28 is a lovely little game shell.

20-GAUGE

The 20-gauge is a big step up from the 28-gauge. It offers about 50 percent less recoil with most loads than the 12-gauge, and even with the heaviest buckshot loads about 40 percent less. While I prefer the 12-gauge, logic dictates that anyone who can shoot the smaller 20-gauge better than the harder-kicking 12-gauge is a well-armed individual; someone who concentrates their practice time on the handgun and the rifle and only occasionally fires the shotgun might find the 20-gauge a far better choice for occasional use.

The 12-gauge can teach you more about flinch and sore shoulders than you ever wanted to learn if you begin without the proper technique. Just the same, I am an experienced trainer and shooter, and the test program with the 12-gauge was sometimes daunting. Flinching and jerking are terrible detriments to accuracy. I have learned to control flinch, but not the need to soak the wrist and massage the shoulder after an intensive training session.

Winchester's No. 3 Buckshot load is a good choice in 20-gauge.

If you too find long sessions on the range with a 12-gauge put you in need of Advil afterwards, I'd advise what I call the "logic ladder." A smaller payload of buckshot that hits the target in the right place when you need it to is superior to a heavy load that misses or isn't properly centered. For teens, a slightly built female, or a senior, the 20-gauge will protect with less recoil than even reduced-recoil 12-gauge loads.

I supplied my daughter with a 20-gauge Mossberg 500 shotgun for home defense. She fired a box of shells and a few buckshot loads, doing well, and found it enough for her as far as recoil goes. That's good, because the 20-gauge is a much better choice for personal-defense than the .410-bore. This is especially true of the magnum 3-inch 20-gauge shell, a formidable loading far more effective than the 20-gauge loads of a century ago. Another

This head shot shows a close-range pattern by Federal's Personal Defense buckshot. The chest shots were made from 15 yards. This is good performance.

bonus: Unlike the 28-gauge, the 20-gauge is actually available in most of the popular pump-action and self-loading shotguns.

16-GAUGE

There are many advocates of the 16-gauge—if you have a Remington 870 in 16-gauge or a Browning Sweet 16 Auto 5, you have a fine shotgun—but even they have to admit that the advantages of the gauge are mostly theoretical. Most problematic, even if you are a fan of the gauge, is that there simply isn't enough selection in factory shells. I did a recent search, and you'd do well to find 16-gauge shells in even some of the best-stocked gun shops.

Hornady's BB shot coyote load is very effective on these varmints. Nickle-plated lead shot offers excellent penetration.

Much development went into improvements of the 12-gauge and the 20-gauge over the years, and even the .410-bore has seen its share of development, as we've seen. The 16-gauge has not enjoyed this attention or improvement.

I hope even the most experienced shotgunner will learn from this book, but this volume is intended primarily to instruct beginners in choosing and mastering the shotgun, especially as it applies to preparation for an emergency (of any scale). I would not recommend choosing a 16-gauge as the shotgun for such emergency preparation, no matter how good the deal or how fine the shotgun.

12-GAUGE

The 12-gauge shotgun is not only the most effective shotgun gauge, it is the most versatile. It may be used for personal defense, hunting small game, and taking many large game animals under the right circumstances. It is suitable for defense against the largest predators in North America, including grizzly bear. You may use the same firearm to hunt squirrels, deer, or boar, and you may pack the shotgun on your back when hiking in bear country. You may take on predators successfully and protect the homestead, and the 12-gauge

Hornady's Critical Defense load is ideal for home defense.

is a formidable personal-defense weapon that can also be used in door breaching and raid scenarios.

My grandfather grew up with the shotgun and taught me its use. I have seen Wilburn Robert Williams take a bushel basket of rabbits, dispatch dangerous animals, and even blow a wasp nest off the outhouse with his 12-gauge! It is the top choice for recreational and competition use.

While some may have more affection for the 16-gauge or 20-gauge, the fact remains that, in modern times, the 12-gauge has gained the most from intelligent development, and as a result, there is much more variety among 12-gauge loads. You can buy "bird bombs," a tool commonly used to frighten birds away from airport runways, and emergency flares can be used in a 12-gauge. There are less-lethal shells, such as those bean-bag and rubber pellet loads often deployed by law enforcement, and there are literally hundreds of choices available across the hunting, target shooting, and personal-defense genres. Walk into a commercial outlet such as Cabela's, and you'll be able to purchase just about any 12-gauge load you desire—and they'll be in plentiful supply, or you may order from an online merchant like Cheaperthandirt. com and let the shells arrive at your doorstep.

Federal Cartridge Company has solved a lot of problems for turkey hunters with a combination load offering both a good open pattern at close range and a tight pattern at longer range with heavier shot.

There are other benefits to the 12-gauge. For instance, the .410-bore and the 20-gauge are often touted as the "beginners" shotguns, but the 12-gauge, by virtue of its more generous pellet payload, may make it easier for many new shooters to actually hit their targets. Too, there are many bargain-basement 12-gauge shotguns on the market that will do a credible job, so if home defense and not serious competition is your goal, you don't have to break the bank acquiring a 12-gauge. While I encourage everyone to purchase the best shotgun they can afford, if you need a shotgun right now the bargain-priced shotguns are attractive. Some, such as the IAC Hawk shotgun, give performance beyond what would be expected for the modest price.

I collected a number of promising 12-gauge loads and tested their penetration through the standard six-inch-wide water jug. The results were impressive.

Winchester's TrAAcker loads may be followed by the eye. The brightly colored wad is visible in flight.

12-Gauge Penetration Testing

Load	Velocity	Average Penetration
Federal 00 Buckshot (reduced recoil)	1,200 fps	20 inches
Hornady Critical Defense	1,505 fps	17.5 inches
No. 4 Buck 2¾-inch	1,250 fps	16 inches
No. 1 Buck	1,090 fps	17 inches
No. 7½	1,349 fps	6 inches
20-Gauge #3 Buck 3-inch	1,150 fps	15.5 inches

Federal's target loads burn clean and offer a great pattern for sporting use. Millions of these rounds have given shooters winning scores.

The author probably fired more Fiocchi birdshot than any other single load in evaluating the shotguns for this book. All around, results have been excellent.

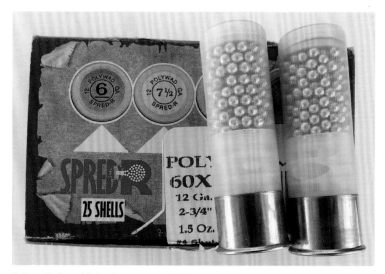

Polywad's Spred-R loads are a wonderful option for up-close small-game hunting.

CHAPTER 6

SINGLE-SHOTS AND THE SIDE-BY-SIDE COACH SHOTGUN

The oldest, simplest, and least expensive shotgun type currently in use is the single-shot, single-barrel shotgun. The double-barrel side-by-side shotgun also sees use, not only as a sporting gun (though the over/under is far more popular for hunting and the clay sports in the US), but particularly for personal defense and farm and ranch duties.

H&R's single-shot is a fun shotgun!

SINGLE-SHOTS

The single-shot shotgun is arguably the last surviving descendant of the muzzleloading shotgun and the Brown Bess rifle. With different sizes of shot, those muzzleloaders were useful for taking different types of game. The modern single-shot is similarly useful.

Though there are a wealth of more modern shotguns to choose from today when it comes to sporting and personal defense, many still like the light, fast handling of the single-shot shotgun and its short receiver; with comparable barrel lengths, the single-shot has a much shorter overall length than a pump-action or semi-auto. The traditional straight stock, break-open action, and hammer-cocking trigger action are simple and robust. Without a mechanical semi-auto action or slide action, the single-shot is also very simple to use and maintain. Really, there's little to go wrong with a single-shot, which is what draws many to keep handy, especially as a firearm of last resort. Because they are often also readily disassembled into two pieces and lightweight, they are also very packable; for emergency situations in which you find yourself on the move, that can be a decided advantage.

Perhaps the biggest audience for a single-shot is the novice shooter. It also finds much use with youth shooters allowed to use a firearm but only when in the company of a mentoring adult. It is an easy firearm on which to train new shooters, and, when in the field, it is easy to make the single-shot safe—simply break open the action.

I often use my H&R break-open 20-gauge as a truck gun. For a quick run in the field to anchor a pesky predator or for small-game hunting, it is a neat, light, and effective shotgun. As a trapper's gun or for anyone trekking where weight is at a premium, again, the single-shot is desirable. Only one warning: single-shots are usually light for their gauge, and that translates to extra recoil. Be certain to fit an adequate recoil pad if you intend to use the single-shot shotgun with heavy loads.

The single-shot shotgun is often found at bargain prices in the used racks of retailers; if the used price is much more than $100, one might well consider upgrading to a pump-action shotgun. A used Harrington &

The single-shot shotgun handles quickly and is light.

Richardson (H&R) single-shot shotgun as I recently found for $75 in the used rack of one of my favorite stores is a useful shotgun.

How relevant is the single-shot today? This past year, I heard accounts of a well-worn single-shot shotgun used at a major airport to launch the "bird bombs" that scare away flocks of birds and keep them from flying into aircraft engines. Another single-shot I know of was

The single-shot is easily made safe by simply opening the breech.

used on a fishing boat to dispatch a large shark brought in with the rest of the catch. And a few years ago, a military advisor told me that the single-shot shotgun is a popular weapon for guards and sentries in many South American nations.

The slim and handy single-shot has much utility.

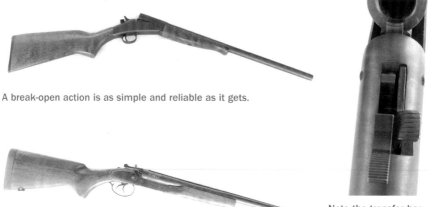

A break-open action is as simple and reliable as it gets.

Traditional styling and modern steel make for a useful combination.

Note the transfer bar safety of the H&R shotgun.

THE SIDE-BY-SIDE COACH SHOTGUNS

I am reminded of the images of New York City detectives armed with double-barrel shotguns decades ago. The side-by-side with its two loads of buckshot was ideal for taking dangerous felons into custody at gunpoint. An instant second shot coupled with the gun's excellent handling qualities allowed these firearms to fill a real need. A correspondent tells me his western police department kept double-barrel shotguns in 20-gauge until at least the 1980s. For making felony arrests in tight quarters, these were formidable firearms.

The double-barrel side-by-side shotgun is also an excellent sporting shotgun. For personal defense, its benefits are that they handle quickly and point well, especially when its barrels are shortened to 18 or 20 inches (sporting lengths run from 24 to 30 inches). The side-by-side isn't well suited for tactical use by special teams, due to its inherent low capacity, but for home-defense, the short-barreled double offers many of the same benefits as the single-shot: safe when broken open, maneuverable, light weight, transportable, and easily handled.

The double-barrel side-by-side is as simple to use as a single-shot. Simply break open the action, load the shells, and close the action. Most modern side-by-sides have internal hammers, though many of today's coach

The Century International Arms Coach Gun has eye appeal.

Dual triggers and external hammers are the hallmarks of the "rabbit ear" shotgun.

When the breech is open, the shotgun is safe.

gun replicas have external "rabbit ear" hammers that must be cocked before firing. Some of these rabbit-ear hammers are to preserve traditional looks and for use in Cowboy Action competition, where Old West authenticity is required of the firearms used. With these, I recommend cocking only one hammer at a time until you are very familiar with the shotgun's handling.

Another advantage of the coach gun is that, with two barrels available, you can "stage" the loads; a lighter load fired first that could do the trick, but then followed by a round of buckshot for more stubborn problems. Too, loads may be changed quickly if the problem is a dangerous animal such as a rattlesnake just outside the door or a predator such as a coyote farther away. In urban settings, the coach gun's maneuverability accommodates the tight hallways and small rooms of many multi-person dwellings (though ammunition choice much be carefully considered so as not to over-penetrate into adjacent apartments). There is also the appeal of the shotgun as a low-key defensive shotgun that doesn't have much negative connotation—the double-barrel is about as politically correct as a shotgun can be. We wish we did not have to consider this, but sometimes we do.

The double-barrel is fun to shoot and can be made useful for many chores. As an example, my old Springfield double-barrel converges the two shot loads on the same spot at 20 yards and does the same with slugs. Two loads of Winchester buckshot will cover the other at 20 yards if I do my part. Slugs are wonderfully accurate to the same distance.

The hammers are cocked in this illustration.

Note the manual safety on the tang of this modern coach gun.

These two cavernous chambers hold 20-gauge shotgun shells.

This makes it suitable for close-range bird hunting, predator dispatch around the homestead, home defense, and even a round of skeet.

The hammers are cocked, as the shotgun is brought to bear on a target.

This coach gun features a pretty nice rib and bead front sight.

At close range, the coach gun would serve for flushed birds at close range, but it isn't ideal for general hunting.

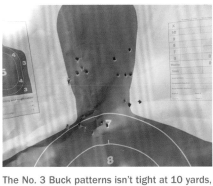

The No. 3 Buck patterns isn't tight at 10 yards, but will do for home defense.

The coach gun handled quickly.

The coach gun is a formidable home-defense shotgun, but also proved to be a really fun gun to shoot recreationally.

Century International Arms' Coach Gun

I have tested the Century International Arms JW2000 extensively. My personal Century Arms double-barrel is a 20-gauge. Also available in the hard-hitting 12-gauge, I elected for the 20-gauge so that everyone in the family could use the shotgun well. The 20-gauge kicks about half as much as the 12-gauge and carries about 55 percent of the payload.

This is a neat little bead-sighted shotgun that handles well. The hammers are not difficult to cock and the triggers are crisp enough. The hinged action was stiff at first, but became easier to use with a couple of trips to the range. This break-in period seems common to the breed. You may have to break open the shotgun using your knee for leverage, when the shotgun is new, but the motion gets easier the more the shotgun is used. Overall length of my Century Arms is 37 inches and it weighs about 7.5 pounds. The action is compact and the barrels are 20 inches long. The choke is open Cylinder on both barrels, well suited for home defense but not for hunting at anything past 20 yards with birdshot. The shotgun handles quickly and gets on target fast.

Most of the shells I've fired have been Winchester's No. 7½ birdshot. This is a great training load, as recoil is light. While I use birdshot for training, in my opinion it is not the best choice for personal defense. At best, birdshot will penetrate only a few inches of testing gelatin, and I believe it would probably be stopped by heavy winter clothing. On the other hand, Winchester's No. 3 Buck load holds 20 large buckshot pellets. This load consistently offers a minimum of 12 inches of penetration in my testing and should cancel Christmas for the bad guys at typical home-defense engagement.

With the open choke barrels of the Coach Gun, 15 yards is the limit for retaining a good pattern. For longer range, the Hornady 20-gauge Lite Slug is a great choice. Even though it's intended for use in rifled barrels, it offers formidable accuracy and penetration at ranges longer than 25 yards.

CHAPTER 7

A PUMP-ACTION PRIMER (AND THE AUTHOR'S FAVORITES)

There are many shotguns and shotgun types that have merit. The humblest shotguns will put food on the table and save your life. But I am going to make a bold statement, one grounded in much personal observation and fact: For personal defense and all-around tactical use, the pump-action shotgun is the best choice. The pump-action is the only type of shotgun proven in combat in the Philippines, World War I, World War II, Korea, Vietnam, and every other war of modern recollection, including our most current conflicts. Indeed, the pump-action shotgun has been in constant use with our troops since 1900.

Maintenance means a lot to any firearm, but a dirty pump shotgun will work when a dirty self-loader will not. Per my testing, I should add that a

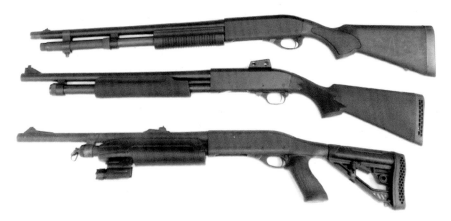

Pump-action shotguns are available in many configurations. Most are very reliable firearms.

dirty semi-automatic shotgun will work if properly lubricated, but it will not run dry. The pump-action shotgun will.

The pump-action shotgun is sometimes called a "slide-action" shotgun. The pump falls into the category of "manually operated firearms," along with bolt-action and lever-action firearms. The bolt-action shotgun had its day and was popular for a brief period. The lever-action shotgun is both immensely complicated and intriguing, as well as a historical artifact of great interest. But it is the pump-action shotgun that has remained, easily the most formidable and reliable shoulder-fired defense weapon ever invented.

The pump gun is reliable in hard use, and it provides for multiple shots, certainly something that can be a benefit if taking game becomes necessary to your survival or you find yourself defending home and family against multiple attackers. Although the majority of pump shotguns hold four shells in the magazine, extended magazines may contain six, seven, or even more. Additionally, with little effort, the pump-action shotgun may quickly be topped off with more ammunition—simply thumb a shell

IAC's Hawk shotgun is inexpensive, but provided faultless performance. It is definitely a best buy.

Adaptive Tactical's fore-end and stock gave this old Remington 870 improved handleability.

The Remington Express Tactical shotgun is a great self-defense weapon available at a modest price.

into the magazine, something a practiced shooter can do without removing the gun from the shoulder.

Flexibility is another hallmark of the pump-action. Such a firearm may have its magazine loaded with light birdshot, followed by a heavy buckshot load and then a medium target load and the shotgun will function without disruption. That is not always the case with semi-automatics. Some semi-autos may be set for different loads, but many have to be partially disassembled in order to do so. (The self-compensating Remington 1100 is an exception to this.)

The Remington 870 pump-action remains the standard by which all others are judged.

SHOOTING THE PUMP-ACTION

To shoot the pump-action, you'll first load the magazine, inserting each shell through the bottom of the receiver against the follower in the magazine tube and pushing it forward until it's retained in the tube. When the magazine is fully loaded, the fore-end is then pulled to the rear. This releases a shell from the magazine onto the carrier (also called an "elevator") and opens the bolt.

The Remington action is fast, no question there.

Slide the fore-end forward, and the shell on the carrier is loaded into the chamber, the bolt closing and locking as it does. The totality of this motion also cocks the internal hammer and preps or resets the trigger, so immediately engage the firearm's safety. Finally, to be fully loaded, you'll then add one more round to the magazine.

In this illustration, the pump-action is racked to the rear and the action is open, bolt to the rear.

Once the pump-action is fired, the action unlocks. You'll cycle the fore-end rearward again, this time ejecting the empty hull as another round from the magazine moves onto the carrier in preparation for chambering the next shot.

The pump-action can be very fast in trained hands. With the shotgun properly shouldered and a firm hold on the fore-end, recoil upon firing helps the user operate the action. The recoils slightly lifts up the barrel, helping the user rack the fore-end to the rear. The fore-end shucked forward in turn helps brings the shotgun back on target. When shooting the pump-action, it is important to have a solid back-and-forth motion with the fore-end, one without slop, as uneven force on the fore-end can result in greater wear on the action.

Some claim that fast fire with the pump-action and the self-loader is practically equal. I tend to agree, though some claim the pump-action is actually faster. Suffice it to say, the pump-action shotgun is more than sufficient to meet any emergency, whether a home invasion by a gang or facing a large and deadly wild animal.

Shells are thumbed into the magazine one at a time.

Another benefit to the pump-action is that it can be easily loaded one shell at a time through the ejection port. (This may also be done when first loading the shotgun, although I prefer the safer method of loading the magazine first.) A trained individual facing a threat will be able to load the chamber through the ejection port quickly if the shotgun runs dry (i.e., you've shot it until it's empty). Simply lock the bolt to the rear by sliding the fore-end all the way back, drop a shell in the port, and rack the fore-end forward.

The pump-action may be chamber-loaded if desired, rather than racking the action to shift a round from the magazine up into the chamber.

This can be much faster in an emergency than trying to thumb a shell into the magazine from the bottom of the receiver.

The fore-end is operable via its operating bars or rails. These action bars are of solid steel and durable. These action bars should be a pair. There have been a few reliable and worthwhile shotguns with single operating bars, but the most reliable modern actions use twin operating bars. The action will be smoother and there is far less chance of a short-cycle—in which you'll fail to fully eject the empty hull, or you'll eject the empty hull but fail to move a shell onto the carrier from the magazine—or other malfunction. I have handled and fired some of the bargain-priced, single-rail shotguns, and they are far from impressive. I find their fore-ends are loose and rattle and the actions are sloppy. That's not something that gives much pride of ownership, and doesn't give the owner confidence the piece will survive in the long-term. There are good affordable pump-action shotguns, as we will see, but beware of those that are too cheaply made.

THE SELF-DEFENSE CHOICE

The pump-action shotgun may be kept at home ready with just the magazine loaded and instantly ready for action. Simply rack the fore-end and you are ready for a shot. It can also be stored safely fully loaded, with a full magazine, a round in the chamber, and the safety on, but you must be diligent in securing this gun (or any gun that is partially loaded or has its ammunition supply unsecured), from use by unauthorized persons. (I'll have more on unauthorized persons in Chapter 14.)

There are those who feel that the noise associated with the racking of the slide is terribly frightening to an assailant and may result in them quickly leaving the premises, at least for the moment. There is some truth in this— but it's mostly an artifice of Hollywood. Hearing a pump shotgun being racked may very well send the everyday criminal on their way. Or it may not. Counting on the noise of a racked slide to thwart the "average" criminal is *never* a good move. It's like holding a cap gun in the dark or a banana in your pocket and hoping they'll think the threat is real. And when it comes to those who are true psychopaths, those who rape, kill and otherwise cause physical harm for enjoyment? Those are a different type of criminal. Such damaged persons aren't going to be stopped if they don't see in your eyes and your actions the willingness to use your firearm. They will disarm you if you are hesitant and use it against you. If you keep a firearm, any firearm, for self-defense, you must be prepared to use it, both mentally and by being properly trained (more on that also in Chapter 14).

This is a rather nice Mossberg .410-bore field gun. It competed with several other shotguns for the fun gun of the year title.

Proper training is what provides confidence to the mental side of being prepared to use your firearm in a life-or-death situation. With pump shotguns, much of this training will focus on how you operate the fore-end. A trainer once told me that his agency switched to a self-loading shotgun because recruits were firing their pump-

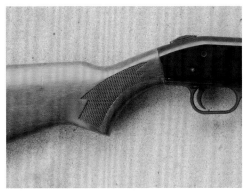

This field-grade Mossberg features excellent wood.

action shotguns and forgetting to rack the slide and reload after firing! I asked how often they trained, and he replied about once a year.

To my way of thinking, the self-loader requires more, not less, training, but then I am not a bean counter or agency administrator. After firing a pump-action shotgun, the bolt is unlocked, and it is a natural reaction to simply rack the action. The shouldered shotgun allows excellent leverage for this motion. But training once a year won't teach you that. My advice: If a pump shotgun is your self-defense choice, practice often.

The Mossberg safety location is superior, the author feels.

EVEN THE TOUGHEST HAVE THEIR MOMENTS

Most of my experience with pump-action shotguns is related to tactical models and riot guns with simple bead sights and short barrels. I have learned a great deal about these shotguns over the years, and I have to admit that, if issued either the Remington 870 or the Mossberg 500, I would be happy with either and concentrate on mastering it. I cannot imagine anything that could be done with one that cannot be done with the other.

That said, as you become better acquainted with your firearms, particularly those you keep for self-defense, you'll need to understand that any firearm can become damaged. If you use them and train with them, the chances are you will see a failure of some type. This is particularly true with the

Remington's Express gave good results in firing tests.

firearms used in teaching, which see much harder use than most personally owned guns.

If during your training and exposure to different firearms you prefer one model over the other, be certain that your purchase decision is backed by fact and research that attests to the longevity and durability of a particular brand and model. As a young cop, I broke an action pin in a particular firearm when firing the piece as quickly as I could cycle the action. That failure soured me for a time on the brand. But the truth was, I'd really abused the piece and it broke. A few years later, the trigger group in the other brand I liked fell apart during a training exercise. Hard use does those things, and, at the time, some of the shotguns in use at various agencies were twenty to thirty years old (not to mention the occasional much older Winchester Model 12s and High Standard Flite Kings).

When it comes to firearms, if you buy quality, longevity is almost always assured. Shoot as many brands and models as you can, do your homework regarding their reputations, then your choice, and practice, practice, practice. Following is an examination of Remington and Mossberg pump-action models we tested for this book, which may help guide you to the purchase that works for you.

THE MOSSBERG 500 VS. REMINGTON'S 870—THE TACTICAL SHOOTER CHOICES

There are shotguns less expensive than a pump that will get some chores done, but not all jobs will be done well. For instance, I said in the previous chapter that a double-barrel side-by-side can be a fine choice for home defense and other uses—but it would be ridiculous to attempt much serious tactical training with such a firearm. Face it, you have two shots and you're out unless you have cover to reload and an ample supply of ammunition. So, when in dire straits, to be all you can be, the pump-action shotgun is demanded.

For me, the choice usually boils down to the Remington 870 or the Mossberg 500. These are the two most popular shotguns in the country, for good reason. While I would hesitate to state one is better than the other, one may be better for one specific shooter than the other.

Each shotgun has an enviable reputation, but the Remington's is the longer, as the 870 was introduced in 1951, ten years before the Mossberg 500; the original Mossberg did not use dual action bars, but was later upgraded. Each brand rates equally as far as the force needed to operate the fore-end and the smoothness of the action. Multiple barrel lengths and choke tubes are available for each. And both are well proven not only in police use, but in military combat the world over. There are differences, however.

I think that many feel that the Mossberg has the superior safety location, but right-handed shooters find either model useful. The Mossberg's tang-mounted safety is ideal for tactical shooters who train shooting from both shoulders. I own both in different configurations and would find my shooting life diminished without either of these shotguns.

The differences between the Express price leader and the standard 870 are slight.

A keen eye will spot the dual extractors of the Mossberg. The Remington 870 has a single extractor. While the single extractor works, and works practically every time no matter what

Remington uses a lever by the triggerguard to unlock the bolt.

the load, the dual extractor would seem superior. My sources tell me they have seen malfunctions with the Remington only when cheap, off-spec shells are used; the Remington extractor will jump over the rim on the rarest occasion. Recently, I suffered a problem with my Mossberg. It would not operate with a certain foreign shell that the Remington readily digested. Still, I have fired many shotguns over forty years or more and have seen very few malfunctions with these two brands.

The Remington receiver is steel, which is a big deal to many of us. However, the Mossberg's aluminum receiver might also be seen as more modern. Aluminum isn't as strong as steel, but the Mossberg will still take just as many magnum firings as the Remington, that is certain. The Mossberg is also slightly lighter and usually less expensive in comparable models than the Remington. Each has excellent aftermarket support in stocks, barrels, and tactical accessories.

The controls of each are simple. There is a trigger, manual safety, and bolt-release button.

The bolt release of each is more or less equal, each loads easily enough, and each magazine may be unloaded using the shell stop.

The Remington safety is mounted in the trigger guard. It is very fast and positive—providing you are right-handed. The Mossberg features a tang-mounted safety. This arrangement is superior for most right-handed shooters and a must for left-handers. This difference in the safety controls may make or break the choice. Let's take a closer look at a model from each of these two brands that I favor and have tested extensively.

MOSSBERG 500C/505 YOUTH MODEL 20-GAUGE

My personal neat little shotgun is marked 500C just above the loading port. A similar model is listed as the 505 in the current catalog, sometimes called the Youth or Bantam model. This is a scaled-down Mossberg 500 with features intended to give short-statured shooters a good fit. The stock is a bit shorter than the full-size shotgun, but the best feature is the EZ Reach fore-end. This fore-end is positioned on the gun to be closer to the shooter than it is with most other shotguns. For me, getting used to it took some time.

The action is short, fast, and very smooth. When I first started with it, I initially overworked the action, which it did not need. This Mossberg 500 has the standard features of other Model 500 pumps, including dual action bars and dual extractors. The 20-gauge version I purchased used at an attractive price also features a rib with dual sighting beads, a nice touch for the money. The wood is well finished and the stock and fore-end are a nice fit overall. The wood may be birch, and while "nicely figured" doesn't come to mind to describe this furniture, it works well and isn't unattractive.

The Mossberg's magazine holds five 2¾-inch shells. If facing a takeover robbery or a team of assailants, this is a good reserve of ammunition. For personal defense, I would load these five shells rather than four 3-inch shells.

The 20-gauge Mossberg isn't as heavy as the 12-gauge pump-action shotguns tested (next chapter), and it handles more quickly. It isn't quite as fast to the shoulder as a single-shot shotgun, but it also kicks less than one.

When firing this Mossberg 20-gauge, some of my testing crew used to other shotguns forgot to let the trigger reset. You cannot ride the face of the trigger; there is a solid reset with this shotgun. Get the rhythm correct, pump the action with its short stroke, and this is a very fast shotgun to shoot.

While I am primarily concerned with personal defense in this book, the Mossberg pump would be a fine field gun for small-game hunting. The Mossberg accepts screw-in choke tubes, though there was only one Full choke supplied with the used gun I purchased. My shotgun performed well with Winchester buckshot loads, giving an excellent pattern.

A synthetic stock version with length-of-pull spacers will be an option for some, especially young shooters with room to grow. It is the shotgun I would recommend for beginners. A teen gifted with this shotgun would find it a valuable heirloom suited to a lifetime of use. An old man like myself found it a pleasant break from heavy, harder-kicking 12-gauge shotguns.

REMINGTON EXPRESS TACTICAL 12-GAUGE

This is an affordable version of the Remington 870 shotgun, one with a bead front sight. Purchased new, it is available with the standard Express or economy-line synthetic stocks, and also with the tactical recoil brake of more expensive shotguns. A set of ghost

The Remington Express fore-end is slim but useable.

Remington's 12 -gauge Express Tactical is a useful shotgun.

ring sights and the muzzle brake add about $150 retail to the Remington, per my research.

Controls and action are the same as with other Remington 870 shotguns. The matte finish is evenly applied. The fore-end is the skinniest of the Remington shotguns with which I have experience, but worked fine in all of my testing; I simply would have preferred more gripping surface. The trigger action is the nicest of the three Remington shotguns I have on hand, pulling at 4.5 pounds—no need for a trigger job on this one.

All that fired the shotgun agreed that the simple front bead was plenty fast to get on target during rapid-fire combat shooting at seven, 10, and 15 yards. At useful buckshot range, the pattern was well centered. The muzzle brake may have helped with recoil, but I was testing Federal Personal Defense and other reduced-recoil loads, and that helped as well. The muzzle brake is removable.

Even though the Remington Express features only a bead front sight, I like to test shotguns with slugs as well as buckshot, and the bead can compromise accurate slug shooting. When moving to the Fiocchi slugs, the results were interesting. Perhaps the light trigger gave an advantage, but at 15 yards excellent results were had, with two slugs in one ragged hole. Not quite the same group as the rifle-sighted shotguns, but for practical purposes, this bead-sighted gun is good to go with slugs at 15 yards. The slugs also struck to the point of aim.

The Remington Express Tactical stock is slightly thicker than the stocks of some other shotguns tested, but not enough to make a difference in handling that I could discern. The recoil pad is solid, versus the vented pads of the other shotguns. The six-round magazine is another advantage I really like.

This would be a better shotgun with ghost ring sights, as the bead front sight limits application at longer range. Still Remington's price leader gave good results and you will have to spend a significant amount of money for more features.

Remington's Express Tactical uses a muzzle brake that is also a choke tube, a nice touch in an inexpensive shotgun.

Interchangeable choke tubes are a big plus in this Remington Express Tactical.

CHAPTER 8

PUMP-ACTION SHOTGUNS AS FAR AS THE EYE CAN SEE

In the last chapter, I covered two high-quality, sturdy, and reliable shotguns that are my personal favorites. But there are dozens of pump-action shotguns out there, and I and my test team put several of the better-known models through their paces. What we found may surprise you. More importantly, they all give you options when it comes to assessing your shotgun needs for personal defense.

MOSSBERG MAVERICK 88

The Maverick 88 is Mossberg's entry-level shotgun designed to compete with imports. In a mind-boggling move, Mossberg moved the safety to the trigger guard in Remington fashion. The trigger guard is fashioned from plastic. I realize this is an economy shotgun, but Mossberg eliminated one of the primary advantages of its shotgun in changing the safety.

Note the Maverick's shotgun safety. It is similar to Remington's.

The Maverick isn't a high-quality shotgun and, in the author's opinion, is inferior to the parent company's Mossberg 500.

I have seen quite a few Mavericks both new and used in the shops for sale. The action bars do not seem tight and the fore-ends rattle. A used Remington 870 or Mossberg 500 is a far better choice than the new Maverick. In my opinion, the Maverick is a shotgun that should be avoided. There are better choices in this price range. I included mention of it here because we tested it and because so many of them are available.

WINCHESTER MODEL 1300 12-GAUGE

The Winchester Model 1200 first saw production in 1964. This low-cost shotgun was well received and eventually adopted as one of several pump-action shotguns issued by the US Army and saw use in Vietnam. By all accounts, it remained in use until at least the 1980s. Some of the military Model 1200 12-gauge shotguns featured a ventilated

The bolt of the Winchester 1300 is a strong design.

handguard, swivels for mounting a sling, and even a bayonet lug. This shotgun was the logical evolution of the Winchester 1897 Trench Gun. The 1200 was available in many configurations, including the Riot Gun, the Buck Special with iron sights and a slug barrel, a 30-inch Full choke turkey gun, and the most common 28-inch barreled sporting gun. The majority were manufactured in12-gauge, followed by 20-gauge and a lesser number of 16-gauges. The sporting guns featured the Winchoke removable choke tubes pioneered by Winchester and featured a four-shell magazine capacity.

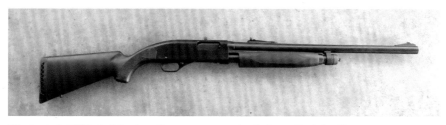

Winchester's 1300 slug gun has given yeoman service in the author's family.

With clean lines and excellent performance, the Winchester 1300 slug gun certainly should be considered for emergency preparedness use.

An important distinction between the Winchester Model 1200 and other shotguns is its rotary bolt head. Hell-for-strong, this bolt head features four lugs that lock solidly into the barrel extension.

The Winchester Model 1300 came next, introduced in 1980–1981. (At this point, Winchester was renamed the United States Repeating Arms Company after Winchester Olin ammunition and

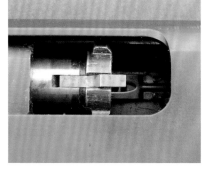

Note the locking bolts of the strong Winchester 1300.

Winchester Repeating Arms became separate entities. Today it is once again Winchester Repeating Arms.) It was a popular shotgun, although it ranked behind sales of the Remington 870 and the Mossberg 500 shotgun. The shotgun was also advertised as the "Speed Pump," as the action is fast—*very* fast—and a trained shooter can rapidly rack the smooth Winchester action. The Model 1300 also got an improved five-round magazine.

The Winchester 1300 has dual action bars, an aluminum receiver, and barrels with choke tubes. An open Cylinder choke Riot gun and versions with a rifled slug barrel were also produced.

The Winchester 1300 went out of production in 2003, but they're a viable used option. The version tested for this report is a late-1990s production slug gun with credible fit and finish given its age. The locking lugs of the bolt are sharp and show little wear, and the rotary bolt locks up tight. The slug barrel features sharp rifling.

I proceeded to test the shotgun with the slugs it was designed for, but I also tested it with buckshot. It is well-known that slug barrels are not compatible with buckshot loads, something confirmed in my testing. Using Winchester's 12-gauge 3-inch Magnum 00 Buckshot load of 15 pellets, the

Winchester 1300 slug gun put its payload into a 13-inch circle at 10 yards. While not hopeless for home defense, this isn't ideal by any means.

Next, I tried the Winchester 2¾-inch military-grade shell. Loaded with nine pellets of 00 Buckshot, this is the defense load standard by which all others are judged. The pattern I got was nine inches at 10 yards, with only eight pellets impacting the target. This confirms that slug barrels are not well suited to buckshot. This isn't a specific fault of the Winchester; the same performance will be demonstrated with any slug barrel you care to test in any brand.

Moving to slugs, I loaded the shotgun with the Winchester 2¾-inch 7/8-ounce shells. At 25 yards, I found the Winchester would print two shells touching the other and the third an inch away. This was outstanding performance, so I moved the target to the 50-yard line, thankful this shotgun wore rifle sights. Taking aim, I fired three Lightfield 2¾-inch slugs. The result was a very neat two-inch 50-yard group.

In my opinion, the Winchester 1300 is a viable shotgun, out of production but available used at bargain prices. I would not turn down a good find in a retailer's used gun rack. (For those who need something new, the design lives on in modern FNH pump-action shotguns.)

BENELLI NOVA TACTICAL PUMP

Benelli has a reputation for high quality, and its Nova has earned high marks quickly. At present, the Benelli is my No. 1 tactical pump kept at ready for alarms and excursions.

The author has great confidence in his Benelli Tactical shotgun.

The Nova's bolt is actuated by dual bars set in the fore-end and leading to the action the same as any other pump-action shotgun. The action is remarkably tight and smooth in my gun. The serrations on the grip and fore-end make for a good grip and provide positive adhesion when firing. The fore-end can become loose with thousands of

The Benelli Nova Tactical handles and shoots well.

shells fired. Simply retighten the fastening nuts.

The Benelli has several excellent features. The version I use is supplied with a good set of ghost ring sights. These sights are well designed, durable, and offer fast hits on target. There are also versions with rifle-type open sights, but the ghost ring sights are much superior for all-around use. It is easy to sight-in the shotgun with slugs thanks to these sights.

Other features include a magazine cut-off on the fore-end. Simply press the button in the stock and this stops feeding from the magazine. This lets the user open the action and feed a slug or other special shell directly into the receiver and address a changing threat or scenario. This is a rather specialized advantage, but nice to have. The button pops back out as the fore-end is moved forward.

Another advantage is the loading port, which is larger than on other shotguns. It is also very easy to load the magazine, something made even easier by the shell carrier design. With the Benelli's carrier, you press it in and it stays locked to the top, allowing unimpeded loading of the magazine.

As for performance, the shotgun performed well during training exercises. For the purposes of this review, I fired the Benelli Nova with Federal Personal Defense buckshot, which produced tighter than average patterns.

Benelli's ghost ring sights are a big advantage on the tactical model.

I also fired a number of Federal TruBall slugs. True to form, the Benelli turned in excellent results with these slugs.

All around, this is a first-class pump-action shotgun that will give you an edge. The only drawback is that the stock is one piece, which makes it

The Benelli safety is well situated for rapid manipulation and positive in operation.

impossible to retrofit with aftermarket stocks and related accessories. That aside, for what it is, the Nova is a great shotgun.

IAC HAWK 982

With the availability of the IAC Hawk, there is no reason to purchase an inferior shotgun. The Hawk is inexpensive, but in every example I have tested, it functions and performs well.

Still, it is difficult for me to give a blanket recommendation to this pump, because I have used only two examples. I do have a friend who has sold over a dozen in his shop, all with good feedback, but I have not seen this gun at 3-Gun competition, where use is hard, nor have I seen an example that has been fired with more than 300 full-power shells.

Ghost ring sights are an excellent addition to any combat shotgun.

What I have seen is impressive and comparable to the Remington 870 in performance. This is because the Hawk is a copy of the 870, with no deviation I can find. The slide action, safety, bolt release, and trigger are the same in appearance and function. Fit and finish are good. The blue is attractive and evenly applied. The trigger breaks at a clean six pounds.

The Hawk features a five-round magazine and synthetic furniture. The stock is slightly thinner than synthetic furniture on Remington's Express Tactical. The Hawk features a vented recoil pad.

I like the sweeping design of the fore-end on the Hawk better than the one on the Remington Express. The hand isn't going to slip off the rear of this fore-end. The real advantage of the Hawk 982, especially in this price range, was the aperture or ghost ring sights. This sight is adjustable and features solid wings to protect it from falls (riot guns tend to get beat up.) The front post is well suited to all-around use with buckshot or slugs. The action is smooth and free from binding.

The only difference I could find in the Hawk and the Remington actions is that the shell carrier of the Hawk does not have the small cutout in the carrier that Remington employs today to inhibit short cycling.

For a little over $200, the Hawk has given good results when firing a number of mixed shells. I began with Winchester No. 7½ birdshot and Fiocchi Golden Turkey field loads, then continued to buckshot and slugs. There were no malfunctions of any type while firing some 200 mixed shells.

In addressing targets at seven, 10 and 15 yards, the Hawk proved excellent. At all ranges, the ghost ring sights gave an advantage in speed. Slug performance was particularly good.

I am impressed with the IAC Hawk 982. The shotgun performed flawlessly. It handled quickly, and the recoil pad design was praised by all raters. The ghost ring sights are ideal for personal defense, and the rear sight may be removed if you wish to mount a red dot sight or other optic.

HARRINGTON & RICHARDSON (H&R) PARDNER (STEVENS PERSONAL DEFENSE SHOTGUN VARIANT)

I was able to test a sporting version of the Pardner with a 28-inch ribbed barrel. The Pardner cost $30 more than the Mossberg Maverick, which is significant in this price range. With an MSRP of $199, the Pardner is occasionally on sale for a bit less. During my testing, each was on sale at Academy Sports, so I was able to compare the shotguns side by side. I like the Pardner better.

The Pardner is a "captive import," marked with the moniker of a big name concern but made in

The H&R-marked import was a nice shooter.

China. The Pardner features a dull blue finish, and the barrel and the receiver are slightly different in color.

The action of the Pardner is a copy of the Remington 870 pump-action shotgun. The internal similarity is striking, although externally the Pardner features a distinctive hump at the back of the receiver. Though the Pardner is an entry-level shotgun, it is of all-steel construction. It is a few ounces heavier than the comparable Maverick 88 shotgun. The stock is wood in the sporting version. Its fore-end is tighter than the Maverick's and the fit superior.

The riot gun version is a credible low-budget defense gun. While the Pardner's action is not as smooth as the Hawk or the Remington 870, it is acceptable. The solid rib of the Pardner features only one bead that sits low on the barrel; this is a nice touch on an economy shotgun.

A big advantage of the Pardner that may be a tie-breaker compared to other economy shotguns is the fact that the receiver is drilled and tapped for scope mounts. For the turkey hunter or shooters who like to mount a red-dot optic, this is an advantage.

When testing the Pardner, I fired the Federal Gold Medal light shot load for the most part. This is a first-class target load that gave excellent patterns on the paper. There were no problems in firing some 300 shells over the course of several months. There was no eccentric wear and the finish showed no degradation. While I admit I am a blued-steel-and-walnut man, I appreciate the utility of modern synthetic stocks. Just the same, I could not get used to the plastic and pinned arrangement of the Maverick I fired,

This Chinese shotgun, branded Stevens, gave acceptable results on the firing range.

The long fore-end with deep striations gave good purchase when testing the Chinese-made Stevens pump-action shotgun.

compared to the better construction of the Pardner. I would prefer a Mossberg 500 to either of these shotguns, but in this price range, the Pardner impressed me.

H&R PARDNER RIOT GUN

There is a steady market for personal-defense firearms in the United States, and a shotgun selling for less than $200 but featuring a solid pump-action, an 18.5-inch barrel, and synthetic stock sells very well. That is the premise of the Pardner. I have seen these shotguns sell for less, but I paid $175 for this one new in the box. Considering that the stock is synthetic and there is no barrel rib, this riot gun should sell for less than the Pardner field gun, but go figure.

The action is smooth enough, in fact, smoother than the Pardner field-grade shotgun just reviewed. The riot shotgun features a plain bead front sight, which is just fine for nitty-gritty, close-range defense work. This is the type of shotgun you will wish to keep in the home, the truck, or in camp. A short, fast-handling 12-gauge shotgun is simply a first-class problem solver.

With a five-shot tubular magazine and a reliable pump-action, the short Pardner is an attractive self-defense option. This shotgun has fired less than 100 shells as of this writing, but there have been no failures to feed, chamber, fire, or eject. I have used Winchester's field loads for the most part with this gun to limit recoil's effect on my crew of testers. The shot load is well centered on the bead to 15 yards, about the maximum distance for effective use of buckshot with a Cylinder-bore shotgun. About half of the shells fired in this shotgun have been birdshot, with a number of heavy field loads and some buckshot. I also used a number of the Winchester PDX1 Personal Defense loads with excellent results—controllable, and with a good pattern at moderate range.

I found the short Pardner reliable and smooth in operation. I will not be retiring my Remington 870 shotguns—one has served faultlessly for thirty years and the other for twenty—but this Pardner often rides in my truck. I have also fired a Stevens-marked version of the same shotgun, one that featured a tactical-style stock with pistol grip and

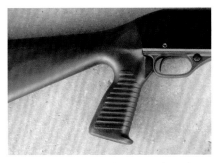

The Stevens pistol grip is ergonomic and proved serviceable during testing.

synthetic furniture and sells for about the same price as the H&R. For the features and price, it is acceptable.

MOSSBERG CRUISER 20-GAUGE

I thought it appropriate to test at least one Cruiser shotgun with its pistol grip. Now, I have deployed the 12-gauge shotgun as a personal-defense gun for many years and seldom thought of any other type, but for Cruiser testing, the 20-gauge Cruiser was chosen. A burly male will find that the 12-gauge pistol grip shotgun is unpleasant and difficult to control. The 20-gauge is easier, but, in the end and in my opinion, this pistol-grip design isn't ideal for most personal-defense use.

I do not have an overblown ego and I do not enjoy firing hard-kicking 12-gauge shotguns, especially those that other members of the family cannot possibly use well. The 20-gauge is a better choice in a gun of this configuration—and far better than the minimally powered .410-bore. The 20-gauge may exhibit noticeable recoil in a lightweight shotgun, but this recoil is generally regarded as half that of the 12-gauge shotgun.

Mossberg's Cruiser shotgun is as reliable as any Mossberg—but the pistol grip configuration isn't for every situation.

The Mossberg is designed for rapid manipulation. The action is smooth and the shell feed positive. The dual action bars work as they should, and I like the tang-mounted safety, which is particularly well placed for use with a pistol-grip stock. The whole package is only 29 inches long and weighs just five pounds. That is light, and the shotgun handles quickly inside close quarters. The scaled-down 20-gauge action is fast, *very* fast.

The author assessing a long-range shot from the Cruiser shotgun.

I prefer a full-stock shotgun as a go-anywhere, do-anything shotgun for personal defense, so in this respect the Cruiser falls short. However, for close-quarters use inside a dwelling or as a truck gun, the Cruiser makes a lot of sense for those willing to practice and master a shotgun of this design.

Patterns should be checked in individual shotguns, of course, but the Winchester buckshot used in my testing showed tight patterns to just past 15 yards. When firing the Cruiser, I was able to get a good hit on the target to seven yards by using both hands and looking at the target, while keeping the bead on the shotgun barrel in the lower part of my vision. It takes practice,

A run on the targets shows it can be done, but it is easier done with a standard full-stock shotgun.

but if you value a shotgun that is easy to stow and deploy quickly, the Cruiser has merit.

WINCHESTER 97

Designed by John Moses Browning, the Winchester 1897 was an immediate success, as were most of his firearms. Though it has been out of production for more than fifty years, there are features of the Winchester 97 that are appealing and make it interesting and viable to today's shooters, so seeking one on a used gun rack isn't something to be overlooked. Too, there are several copies of this famous Winchester shotgun available today. I cannot

The Winchester 97 shotgun was the first with the most!

The Winchester 97 action is proven and seems never to break.

comment on the quality of those copies, but their reputation is that their operation and capabilities are similar to the original.

The Winchester 97 was among the greatest shotguns of its day and a popular improvement over the less than perfect Winchester 93 because this new model used shells with smokeless powder. It featured a smooth and reliable pump-action—even today, tie-ups and short cycles of well-worn 1897 shotguns are rare—and it was made from the best materials available.

The magazine holds five 12-gauge 2¾-inch shells. A difference in the Winchester action and modern shotguns with their magazine disconnects is that the Winchester 97 may be "slam fired" by simply keeping the trigger pressed as the action is worked.

There is no manual safety. Once the Winchester 97 shotgun is loaded, its external hammer may be carefully lowered by hand (with the firearm pointed in a safe direction, of course). Once lowered, the hammer can then be pulled back slightly until it clicks. This is the "safe" position, as the hammer does not touch the firing pin.

The 97 earned an enviable reputation for reliability. Maintenance is simple, though takedown is slightly more complicated than with more modern pump-actions. Still, pressing a button to release the magazine and twisting the barrel out of alignment to remove it isn't difficult.

Results with the author's shortened Winchester were fair. The choke was definitely open Cylinder.

The Winchester 97 was offered in a "riot gun" or short-barreled configuration for most of its production life. Many were used by law enforcement and prison guards, and all were marked Cylinder bore. The most famous was the World War I Trench Gun, but the gun had made a name for itself long before that first great war, and its military use continued at least until Vietnam.

Though long out of production, by all reports the originals hold up well to use. I had the desire for a riot gun variant for personal use. Originals in top condition are pretty pricey, nearing $1,000 or more if the Winchester is a bona fide Trench Gun. I was able to find a sporting model in good condition,

Fiocchi shells in both birdshot and buckshot were tested with excellent results.

one manufactured in 1952, for less than the price of a modern clone. Given its condition, it was a good buy—save for its long barrel. But I had a plan. I took the Winchester to my local gunsmith. Jim asked, "Are you sure to want to do this? This is a nice, original Full choke Winchester." Joyce, my wife, was with me and said, "Live the dream." Well, why not? I'm not a duck hunter. And so

This old Winchester 97 may seem to be falling with every stroke of the handle, but it always works.

the barrel was cut to 18.5 inches—a little shorter than a true trench gun—and the bead reinstalled.

I oiled the shotgun and practiced quite a bit in dry-fire. Acclimation took time. The lockup is different than with other pumps, and in dry-fire you have to really press forward on the fore-end to unlock the action. A small button on the right side of the receiver also unlocks the action. The action also features a single operating bar.

The Winchester 97 was much lauded in its day, but in the final analysis, I found it isn't as smooth as the modern, twin-bar Remington 870. That's really not a surprise, but that isn't the whole story.

I took the Winchester to the range along with a good mix of 12-gauge shells. I began with Fiocchi's birdshot loads for acclimation, then loaded Fiocchi 12-gauge reduced-recoil buckshot. Sure enough, the old gun pointed well and is well balanced. The stock and trigger guard have a different feel than more modern shotguns, but they are still functional.

Next, I tested the slam-fire feature. I tried first with birdshot and kept the butt of the 97 in my shoulder, leaning into the stock to absorb the repeating recoil. Keeping the finger on the trigger, I found I could keep most of the birdshot on the target at seven yards. Moving the stock to be held under the arm and firing was more challenging, but faster. Beginning with the bead on the front center of the target I found that I could fill the target with shot at seven yards and sometimes have two shells in the air at the same time. That is *working* that trombone action!

After this initial testing with birdshot, I loaded Fiocchi buckshot loads. Results were much the same. The Winchester 97 doesn't kick more or less than any other shotgun, and it's a tad heavier than some. It will lay down buckshot like no other shotgun, in my experience.

One note: The Winchester 97 doesn't have a butt pad. I fired three full-power buckshot loads from the shoulder, and the experience was not pleasant. Despite the very cool look of the original buttplate, a shotgun discovered on a used gun rack and put to use for self-defense would need to have a recoil pad installed for comfortable use even with standard loads (not to mention that a rubber pad helps keep the gun on the shoulder).

There are more advanced shotguns with rifle sights and AR-15-style stocks. But for home defense and as a truck gun, the Winchester 97 will do what it always has. This shotgun has a good natural point, handles quickly, and there is little to go wrong mechanically. If you find one used in good condition, snag it.

ROCK ISLAND 12-GAUGE

This shogun is a copy of the old High Standard Flite King. The design and execution seem well done, and the shotgun is often found with a marine finish. This shotgun does not have a removable or takedown barrel, which may be an issue for those looking for a shotgun that packs easily for transport.

The version tested is smooth enough, and a ventilated handguard is a nice touch. However, one of the screws holding the handguard was damaged on my test gun, even though it was new. The stock mates to the receiver well, and the action is a Speed Feed version (or more likely a copy of the Speed Feed).

The Rock Island shotgun functioned fine during the initial evaluation; however, during the test I experienced a failure to feed when a shell hung under the carrier. I do not think I was responsible for this short cycle, and it was the only incident of its kind during our testing. I have no idea how this shotgun would hold up to an active practice regimen. If you can purchase a better shotgun you should, but, for the modest price, the Rock Island shotgun isn't your worst choice.

The economy and entry-grade Rock Island shotgun gave fair to good results on the firing range.

The Rock Island pump-action shotgun in marine finish isn't your worst choice, though there are better.

CHAPTER 9

SELF-LOADING SHOTGUNS

Many shooters prefer the self-loading shotgun, with good reason. Those using Benellis, FNHs, and other highly reliable shotguns often note that there is no chance of short cycling the self-loader, so the type is more reliable than the pump. When a semi-automatic is properly maintained and handled, and it is fired with quality loads, there is much truth in this. They are also softer on recoil than any other shotgun action type, a worthwhile consideration with heavy hunting or self-defense loads. The Mossberg 930 I often use is much more comfortable to fire and use with heavy loads compared to the Mossberg 500 pump, and the same is true of the Remington 1100 compared to the Remington 870. For all but the most skilled pump-action aficionado, semi-autos produce faster follow-up shots, and the self-loading shotgun is both easier to use from behind cover—no need for elbow room to shuck the slide on a pump or break open a single-shot or coach gun for reloading—and by those with some physical disabilities.

The Mossberg 930 proved to be a soft-shooting shotgun.

Some complain that semi-autos are picky, both when it comes to ammunition choices and keeping them clean. That is also true. But I think that some shooters make too much of the time between cleaning or how many shells a semi-auto will take before malfunctioning and then say, "A-ha! I *knew* it would fail!" Make no mistake, peak performance and reliable functioning are absolutely dependent on proper cleaning and lubrication when it comes to semi-automatics. I clean the guns I stake my life on after every practice run.

Firing off-hand the Mossberg 930 was comfortable.

The first successful self-loading shotgun was the Browning A5, patented in 1900 and in continuous production until 1998. Browning now produces a much changed and updated version, one that resembles the original only in the "humpback" receiver design of the original. The original A5 was a durable and useful shotgun, and it's far from uncommon to still see them in the game fields and on ranches and farm. Among the thousands and thousands of production A5s, there have been short-barreled versions suitable for personal defense, including various military and police versions, that can be sourced through online auctions and on retailer's used gun racks.

Let's look at a few others with stand-out designs.

REMINGTON 1100

The Remington 1100's primary claim to fame is in the sporting field, but there are some short-barreled versions that make fine tactical shotguns. If you own a vintage Remington with a longer bird hunting or clay sports barrel, Cabela's offers rifle-sighted barrels that

Remington's 1100 is a fairly light-kicking shotgun.

are easily substituted for your original. Used 1100s are also often available with spare barrels at attractive prices.

The 1100 has been in service since 1963. This gas-operated shotgun seems to just keep shooting with a minimum of maintenance. Incredibly, one noted Remington 1100 fired some 24,000 shells without a single malfunction or parts breakage—and without cleaning. That would indicate that, contrary to most semi-automatics, the 1100 doesn't need to be super clean to function reliably (though it does need to run with lubrication).

The 1100 functions by bleeding off expended gas from a fired round through ports in the barrel near the forward edge of the fore-end. These gases drive an operating action sleeve to the rear, and this pushes the bolt to the rear. A spent shell is ejected and a fresh shell is sent from the magazine to the carrier as the bolt travels to the rear—just like with a pump-action, only the gun's doing the work, not the shooter. In the second half of the cycling, the bolt comes back forward and the new shell on the carrier is lifted into the chamber, ready to fire as soon as the bolt closes. It is a very fast action.

The 1100 was among the first "self-compensating" shotguns. This means that the 1100 will most often run with all standard shells, without interruption or swapping out parts internally. This is unlike the old Browning A5s, which required removing the fore-end and adding or subtracting friction rings to adjust for different shotshell power levels. For instance, an A5 set to function with light target loads would have its action battered by a heavy buckshot load, and one set up to function with buckshot would more often than not fail to cycle enough to even eject an empty hull from a target load. Such a gun is not ideal for emergency or defense situations unless you intend to run only one type of load through the gun and have an ample supply of it.

I tested the Remington 1100 with an interesting new loading from Federal Premium Ammunition. This is a load called the 3rd Degree. According

Note the different sized holes in the target from the formidable Federal 3rd Degree turkey load. The Remington 1100 made firing this heavy load actually pleasant.

to Federal's research, over the years, turkey loads have been engineered to be more effective at longer range, but have become less so at close range. This often results in missed birds for those who call them in close. Federal

Lock the bolt open and lubricate the self-loading shotgun before firing.

already had the Flitecontrol wad, a wad designed to enhance patterns in its other turkey load, in its arsenal of shotgun technologies. To this it added a three-stage payload of multiple shot sizes, each separated from the other in the shotgun shell body. The unique loading produces excellent patterns from minimal distances of 10 yards or so on to 50 or more with the right shotgun

and choke (see the chapter on loads and patterning). The payload consists of 20 percent No. 6 Flitestopper pellets (a specially designed pellet that has both an extended middle "Saturn" ring and is flat on two sides), 40 percent copper-plated No. 5 lead shot and 40 percent heavyweight No. 2 pellets. The pattern likewise is layered, with the smaller shot doing its job at close range, while the heavier shots patterns well at medium ranges and distance. The Remington 1100 I tested has been going for decades, and it fed, chambered, fired, and ejected these super-modern high-tech loads without a problem.

The Remington 1100 bolt release is located in the magazine well.

In the author's opinion, the Remington 1100 is possibly the most reliable semi-automatic shotgun ever made.

MOSSBERG 930

There are several versions of the Mossberg 930. The sporting guns are solidly built designs and offer excellent all-around utility. In the tactical line, upgrades with ghost ring sights can be worthwhile considerations.

The author developed a healthy respect for the Mossberg 930 shotgun.

Of all the self-loading shotguns tested, I liked the 930 the best. The handling, speed into action, the ease with which the bolt is racked via its generous bolt handle, and the seven-round magazine are all features to appreciate. I particularly like the tang-mounted safety.

The best part about the gas-operated Mossberg is its easy shooting. It was the most comfortable shogun tested for this book when firing full-power buckshot ammunition. The 1100 and the FNH are also good shotguns, but the 930 simply shoots most easily of the three with heavy loads. There are concerns with this model that must be addressed, however, and they relate to a standard break-in procedure.

In common with quality AR-15 rifles, the Mossberg 930 must be cleaned before it is fired. This removes heavy packing grease and preservatives. A firearm from a company that produces as many firearms as Mossberg does may be in the distribution system for months before finding itself in the hands of the end user, so some type of insurance against corrosion is needed. The best strategy is to clean the 930 and then lubricate the action before taking it to the range.

At the range, use only full-power loads for the first fifty shells or so. This regimen has given me good results with two 930s. A third came out of the box running, but short-cycled after some fifty shells. That particular fire-arm had heavy packing grease that had worked loose in the action after those

The Mossberg has many intelligent features, including a large bolt handle and the ability to mount an optical sight.

The Mossberg 930 proved reliable with Hornady 12-gauge buckshot.

The Mossberg may be loaded with just one shell in the chamber to get started.

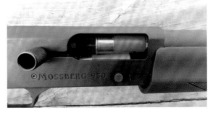

The Mossberg 930 test suffered a troubling double-feed that did not repeat itself.

first rounds had been fired, inhibiting cycling. Another problem (one that isn't unique to the 930) is the shotgun malfunctioning after a shell holder—an accessory many action sports competitors and personal-defense practitioners add to their shotguns to provide up to five extra shells close at hand for fast reloading—has been attached to the receiver. This rather unbalances the gun where it needs to be balanced for proper action cycling. My advice: If you need a shell holder, attach it to the buttstock.

When practicing fast work with the self-loading shotgun, it will be obvious if you are firing too quickly and allowing the muzzle to rise too much during recoil.

The Mossberg 930's ejection pattern is forward of the shooter.

The Mossberg 930 home-defense version proved a to be capable shotgun.

Mossberg's 930 was easily the most comfortable shotgun to fire and use among those tested.

I broke-in the test Mossberg in with 3-inch Winchester 00 Buckshot loads. They are powerful and a really smart choice for a defensive situation, yet, in the Mossberg 930, they are not taxing to the shooter. I have also fired the 930 extensively with Winchester reduced-recoil loads and the formidable Winchester Personal Defense PDX1 loads. The shotgun is comfortable and easy to use with all. I like this one a lot.

FN AMERICA SLP MK 1 TACTICAL SHOTGUNS

The FN America self-loading shotguns are reliable, workmanlike, and well suited to tactical use. The model SLP MK I is a short-stroke, piston-action semi-automatic, similar in action design to the Browning Gold (discontinued in 12-gauge but still available as a 10-gauge), and Winchester Super X2, which are manufactured under the same corporate umbrella. There are two gas ports in this design. When the shotgun is fired, some of the expended shell gases bleed into these two ports. A gas piston is moved, and this pushes the action sleeve and operating rod, which impacts the bolt carrier to push the bolt and carrier to the rear and ejects the empty hull from the fired shot. Then the recoil spring returns the bolt, chambering a new shell from the magazine along the way. This short-stroke system has proven reliable and seems to operate more cleanly than other actions.

The MK 1 is supplied with a pair of gas pistons. One must be used for light loads and the other for heavy loads. They are relatively simple to change out, and a trained user may change pistons in less than two minutes. The rifle-type sights are good and the receiver is drilled for mounting a red-dot sight. This shotgun is supplied with choke tubes. I like this in a tactical shotgun. I prefer a Full choke, which is not supplied, but extra chokes are easily ordered. I have fired several of these shotguns, and they have proven reliable, effective on targets, and fast handling. They simply have no drawbacks.

Although I continue to recommend the pump-action shotgun for most self-defense users and those including a shotgun in their emergency preparedness plans, this is at least partly due to my police experience, when the shotgun was not a personally issued weapon, but rather the community

Some tactical shotguns are complexly designed and accessorized and should be left to special teams of highly trained individuals or competition use.

The FNH semi-automatic shotgun is a great performer overall, and its lack of recoil made shooting more comfortable with heavy loads.

firearm shared by many officers. Those shared guns had to come up shooting every time, and there were rules concerning their storage and the loads deployed. But when working up this chapter, one advantage became more and more obvious: A well-designed gas-operated shotgun exhibits much less felt recoil than the pump shotgun, and that can make a big difference to shooters just getting started and those who can't get comfortable with other, harder-kicking shotguns. The FN semi-auto shotguns are no exception to this. I enjoyed firing the self-loaders more than the pump-action shotguns, and I tended to use heavier loads with the semi-automatics.

TRISTAR ARMS TEC-12

I tend to be "all I can be" with my handguns and rifles, so at some point I realized it was time to step up to a shotgun that offered more than a coach gun or pump. I settled upon the TriStar Arms Tec-12 as my go-to self-loading shotgun. It is affordable in comparison to many tactical shotguns, but it is also reliable and effective.

The Tec-12 bears a striking resemblance to the Benelli M3. (I'd say it is arguably a clone of that shotgun.) It uses the dual-action system that has been successful with the SPAS 12 and Benelli M2 shotguns, in that the action may be changed from self-loading to pump-action by moving a spring-loaded ring just ahead of the fore-end. The primary merits of the system are the ability to

The TriStar Arms Tec-12 was among the most interesting shotguns tested. Performance could not be faulted.

handle light loads the self-loader may not cycle properly, as well as accommodate the launching of special munitions such as flash-bangs and paint markers, all in one firearm. The Tec-12 should can competitive in 3-Gun competition and is a viable self-protection shotgun.

The Tec-12 in semi-auto mode utilizes the proven inertia system of Benelli's shotguns. With all but light target loads, the action never requires adjustment and cycles very quickly. There are three main parts: the bolt body, rotating bolt head, and inertia spring. The inertia system is regarded as the cleanest of systems, versus recoil or gas operation, as no gas or powder residue fowls the action. This means less cleaning and maintenance. When it is time to clean, the shotgun field strips as easily as the Remington 870 pump.

Winchester's sledgehammer PDX1 loads gave first-class performance in the TriStar Tec-12 shotgun.

The action is a strong one, due to steel locking lugs. Yet the lighter mass of the gun's overall parts is what makes for the speed I have seen when firing the shot-

Light loads have a tendency not to function well in tactical self-loaders; just the nature of the beast.

gun. The action has been thoroughly proven in the field by the Benelli M3, and there is no reason this Turkish-built clone gun should not perform in a similar manner.

Most of my Tec-12 testing was done in the self-loading action. I discovered that when birdshot is used in this mode, it will feed and fire, but the empty case will fail to properly eject, resulting in a tie-up. This malfunction and jam take time to correct, which could compromise you in an emergency situation. There are, of course, heavier field loads that will function perfectly in the semi-auto mode, but it will take time to discover which ones work for you every time you pull the trigger. Also keep in mind that on this gun, the pump-action mode is *not* recommended for heavy loads such as magnum buckshot or heavy slug loads. This information taken together means that while this gun offers lots of options, you will have to spend time on the range with various loads to fully understand which

The Tec-12 shotgun feels right and shoots well. It is a reasonably priced tactical shotgun.

operate in which modes and then practice so that you do not confuse loads in an emergency and compromise yourself or the integrity of the shotgun with a load that's not most appropriate for the chosen action.

To switch modes of operation from semi-auto to pump, the action must be closed. Next, you'll locate the selection ring on the fore-end. Move the ring counter-clockwise to disengage the locking ring and pull the fore-end to the rear to change to pump-action. In returning to semi-auto operation, the ring is moved clockwise and the fore-end then pressed forward to re-engage it.

The shotgun's other features include a generous Picatinny rail for mounting a red-dot or other optical sight. Sling swivels are supplied, as well as a removable choke tube. The barrel is 20 inches long. The front sight is a red fiber optic unit, it is shielded from knocks, and offers an excellent aiming reference point. The rear sight is an adjustable ghost ring sandwiched between two protective ears. A straight stock with pistol grip has a solid recoil pad. The trigger breaks at seven pounds. During testing, I discovered the Tec-12 handles quickly and that the pistol grip permits good control during tactical movements.

The TriStar Tec-12, based on a Benelli design, is a fine-performing tactical shotgun.

Loading and firing the shotgun is straightforward. With the bolt closed, the Tec-12 is loaded by thumbing shells into the magazine located under the barrel. If at any time you need to unload the magazine, the spring-loaded shell holder on the left side should be depressed. The magazine holds five 2¾-inch shells or four 3-inch shells. To load a round in the chamber, rack the bolt

The Tec-12 handles well and is ideal for area defense and combat use.

to the rear and quickly release. (Never slowly work the bolt of any self-loader, as this can cause a misfeed.)

The safety is a push-button type in the front of the trigger guard. It is easily manipulated.

The bolt locks open on the last shot in both modes. A button on the right side of the receiver is pressed to release the bolt. Since the bolt locks open after the last shell is ejected even in pump mode, the drills commonly used to load a self-loading shotgun—dropping a shell in the breech and pressing the bolt release to load it into the chamber—remain useful and make training less complex.

I have had experience with self-loading shotguns that were reliable with only full-power loads, as well as others that required changing action rings or gas blocks for reliability. I fired a wide variety of 12-gauge loads in the TriStar shotgun. Reliability was never in question with either full-power buckshot or reduced-recoil loads.

I began in semi-auto mode, with a mix of slugs and buckshot. These included full-power Federal 3-inch slugs, Fiocchi 1-ounce Aero slugs in both reduced-recoil and full-power options, Winchester 3-inch Magnum 00 Buckshot (the hardest kicker), and Hornady's Varmint Express No. 4 Buckshot. The shotgun functioned with *every* load. The action was very fast, with the spent hulls sent spinning in the air after ejection, even with the lighter loads. Recoil was stout with the 3-inch shells, but seemed less brutal than with the pump-action Remington 870 riot gun I normally deploy. The ported choke appears to help control muzzle rise between shots. Patterns seem better than with the average Cylinder choke, and while

I prefer heavier buckshot, the Hornady Varmint Express gave excellent patterns at 15 yards.

Next, I fired the shotgun with a selection of loads I normally keep on hand for use in my personal shotguns. These included the Hornady Critical Defense 00 Buckshot, Fiocchi Aero slug, and Winchester 12-gauge PDX1. The first is a reduced-recoil buckshot load, the second a full-power 1-ounce slug, and the PDX1 is a defense load with a combination of a 1-ounce slug and three 00 Buckshot pellets. I began from the low-ready position (pointed towards the target, but with the buttstock at the waistline), and brought the shotgun quickly to the shoulder, firing a full magazine of the Hornady buckshot loads first at seven yards, then repeating the drill at 10 yards. The 4x7-inch pattern was centered and tight at 10 yards. Recoil was manageable and the action cycled quickly. I next fired two magazines of the PDX1 load, with accuracy that was satisfactory.

I was limited to 20 yards in testing the Fiocchi slug, but accuracy was excellent. The Tec-12 was properly sighted for use at 20 yards and, literally, placed one slug on top of the other; three slugs went into less than two inches.

After this evaluation, I find the TriStar Tec-12 to be an excellent shotgun for defense use. As a truck gun or for protection in the wild, it is a well-designed and capable firearm. Its dual operation modes do require training, but offer benefits a shotgun of solitary action cannot.

Turning this lever allows the user to switch from self-loading to pump operation with the TriStar Tec-12.

TRISTAR RAPTOR ATAC

The TriStar Raptor ATac is a single-mode semi-automatic. There is an obvious family resemblance to its dual-mode Tec-12 sibling.

The Raptor as a personal-defense choice has several nice features. First, it is about a half-pound lighter than the Remington 870. It features a 20-inch barrel and holds five rounds in the magazine. Interchangeable chokes add versatility. Handling is excellent in a close-quarters home environment, with

The Raptor is a simpler shotgun than the Tec-12 and handles well.

In this image, the TriStar Raptor has fired and is unlocking.

the pistol grip allowing secure one-hand carry, although you really need both hands on the gun to hit anything. You aim this one like a rifle.

Function was reliable with full-power shells. With birdshot and other lighter loads, function was problematic, as expected; it ran correctly about 50 percent of the time with mid-power field loads. With full-power buckshot it ran like a charm, never failing to feed, chamber, fire, or eject. After a modest break-in period, it also ran fine with reduced-recoil buckshot and slugs.

I fired this shotgun more than some of the others tested for two reasons. One, the brand is less well-known, and two, it is a self-loading shotgun and

Recoil is always stout with full-power loads, but the self-loading action of the TriStar Raptor soaks up some recoil.

that means reliability had to be qualified. Over two hundred full-power buckshot shells, primarily Wolf and whatever else was cheapest, were fired without incident over extended testing. (Wolf is a good training load as it functions well, but patterns were too wide for personal defense past a very short distance.) I also fired a handful of Winchester, Remington, and Federal reduced-recoil buckshot loads with equally good results. Another forty Wolf 12-gauge slugs were fired, as were twenty-five Fiocchi Aero slugs. The Aero slug is twice as accurate as the Wolf and offers good penetration, while the Wolf fragments early.

This book is primarily concerned with personal defense, but the option to use the Raptor for turkey and other game is important to many of us as well, especially in an emergency severe enough to cause one to hunt their own dinner. In my limited testing to 25 yards, the Raptor was very accurate with the impressive Fiocchi Aero slug, and I feel that it would be a 50-yard deer gun with these slugs. With heavy field loads, turkey can be had. But its failure to function 100 percent of the time with anything but buckshot, slugs, and heavy field loads should discount this one as a go-to do-everything shotgun.

CHAPTER 10

PREMIUM PICKS

There are shotguns that lack traditional looks. Not all have a much practicality, but a few have merit in the realm of self-defense and prepping for worst-case emergencies.

Kel-Tec's KSG is a thoroughly modern and impressive shotgun.

Among the most innovative of these non-traditional creations is the Kel-Tec KSG shotgun. The KSG is unmistakably of modern design and advanced engineering. This is a shotgun in which the user should immerse themselves, learning well its nuances and unique operation if they are to deploy the shotgun for personal defense.

Frankly, as I worked up this book, I wondered if I could do the design justice, as it is so different from every other gun covered. As it turned out, I spent more time with the KSG than any other single shotgun in this book, not because it was troublesome or needed special manipulation, but because it is just so unique.

The KSG is as unconventional in appearance as a shotgun could be. It appears in a bullpup configuration and works as a pump-action with two rails. When shouldered, the receiver is behind the shooter's

The author fitted a TruGlo red dot optic to the KSG and improved his performance with distance work.

The TruGlo red dot improved accuracy with the modern KSG shotgun.

cheek, while the barrel is under the cheek and forward. Its pistol grip is also the backside to the trigger guard. If the KSG bears a similarity to any other shotgun at all, it would be the Ithaca 37, as both share bottom ejection.

The KSG has one barrel and chamber, but two magazines for a total capacity of fourteen 2¾-inch shells, seven in each magazine. With one in the chamber, you have fifteen. The KSG also accepts 3-inch shells, which cut capacity to twelve shells. The magazines feed independently. A lever operates as a stop switch between magazines. Choose which magazine you wish to load and move the lever to cover the other magazine. Load the shells as you would into any other tubular magazine. When the one magazine is fully loaded, move the selector switch to cover it and load the other. This selector also acts as a safety to block both magazines when in the middle position.

Unloaded, the gun tips the scales at seven pounds. Loaded it is 8.5 pounds. It is manageable during fast movement, and you do not notice the gun getting lighter as shells are expended.

The options with a two-magazine setup like this are pretty broad. You can load one magazine with buckshot and the other with slugs, for instance. If you find your adversary is behind cover or farther away than anticipated, simply flip the switch to activate the magazine you feel best addresses the situation.

The KSG takes some getting used to, but after acclimation it offers excellent performance.

Alternately, you could move the lever to the middle position, stop the feeding from either magazine, and drop a slug into the chamber. It isn't as easy to chamber a shell with the KSG as with a standard shotgun, but that's a downside that will be mitigated with training. After a few hours practice with the KSG, I found

The KSG bolt release is quite ergonomic.

myself working the action by second nature. When you run one magazine dry, simply run your firing hand back to the lever and flip it to access the shells in the other magazine. This is the fastest reload I have ever seen! I much prefer the KSG system to the bulky, ungainly, add-on magazines made for the pump shotgun.

The KSG cross-bolt safety is reliable and easy to access.

As I read Kel-Tec's technical description of the shotgun, I realized that the conventional lockwork would be durable, but adapted to a thoroughly modern pump-action shotgun. The receiver is forged steel. The bolt locks solidly into the barrel. Like all pump-action shotguns, the bolt is locked when the action is cocked. A release lever in front of the trigger guard releases the bolt when the bolt is locked. After firing, the hook extractor grasps and removes the spent shell from the chamber. The follower is also an ejector that ejects one shell as the next round is fed onto the shell carrier.

In Kel-Tec fashion, the stock and fore-end are made of glass-reinforced nylon. The grip and fore-end are nicely checkered and provide firm purchase. When handling the KSG, the bolt release and safety are within easy reach. Each is also positive in operation. Another appreciated feature is 12 inches of Picatinny rail on the top of the receiver for mounting optics. The lower six inches of rail afford other options, including a laser or a combat light.

The action is smooth enough, but absolutely demands it be worked forcefully and completely to the rear and back forward if the operator wants to avoid a short-cycle. Keep a steady, firm hand on the fore-end. I think those who report a malfunction or short-cycle with the Kel-Tec KSG are likely going too fast. With so much ammunition available, there is a desire to empty the

The KSG shotgun is well-suited to modern tactical operations.

magazine as quickly as possible, switch to the backup magazine, and fill the air with lead again. That's okay when you're having some fun, but, from a training standpoint, it doesn't correlate well to personal defense. Firing at a reasonable rate and getting a rhythm going results in excellent speed and reliability. As for recoil, I

Kel-Tec's KSG offers plenty of room for mounting red dot sights and combat lights.

had a pleasant surprise—my old Remington 870 riot gun kicks more! (To be fair, the Mossberg with a Magpul stock kicks less.) I cannot readily discern how the KSG dodges recoil, but it does, and what recoil is there isn't at all nasty. If you can handle any other riot-type shotgun, you can handle the KSG.

The only problem I had with the KSG is that I like a more forward grip for better control. There is an optional

Combat-ready, fast-handling, and reliable, the KSG is a great choice for special tactical teams.

vertical fore-grip, and many shooters will find that an ideal solution.

The KSG's18-inch barrel is bored Cylinder, however this Cylinder is a little tighter than others I've worked with. I like that. Federal Personal Defense buckshot load shot an excellent, tight group; at 10 yards, 4x4-inch patterning was common.

Many prefer a forward-handle for cocking the KSG.

A few tips on ammunition for the KSG. First, do not use paper-hulled shotshells, as they are not sturdy enough for this action. Beware of cheap plastic shells as well. Some I tested became bulged at the very top.

I began my evaluation of the KSG with Winchester's No. 9 birdshot. I loaded both magazines and fired my first shots into the berm. The action was smooth, and it wasn't difficult to get fast hits on a man-sized target at 10 yards. I followed with Federal's Personal Defense buckshot load. Recoil was mild and the patterns tight. As for slugs, Federal's TruBall slug posted excellent results. At 10 yards, three shots made a single ragged hole, and I shot a three-shot 1.5-inch group at 25 yards. This dog will run!

Maintenance with a gun this complex is, as you would think, essential to its reliability. To field strip the KSG, verify the gun is unloaded and remove all ammunition from the magazines. Remove the disassembly pins from the buttstock, driving them left to right. The grip assembly may now be removed. Next, the buttstock is pulled to the rear and off the shotgun. The bolt is pulled from the receiver by pulling the slide and lifting the bolt. This is all that is needed before proceeding with routine cleaning and lubrication.

When handling the KSG, think outside the box. It will do things other shotguns will not!

The Kel-Tec KSG isn't for everyone. The occasional shooter may find fun and novelty in it, but the dedicated defensive shooter who masters the techniques associated with a high-performance firearm like this one and learns how to

When the KSG shotgun is taken as a whole, it is specialized, but in that specialization it leaves little to be desired.

properly manipulate the action and quickly change magazine feed will find a unique and formidable firearm like no other.

TRISTAR KRX

A drawback to many shotguns employed for self-defense has been their relative low capacity compared to handguns and rifles. There are some maga-zine extensions available, but

The KRX shotgun is an interesting development, mating AR-15 furniture with a proven shotgun action.

they usually get you to only seven or eight rounds. For those looking for more and who don't desire the bullpup configuration of the KSG, the TriStar KRX is it.

The KRX uses well-made Turkish-manufactured components and operates on the same principles as the Raptor and the Tec-12. Bu the KRX is a self-loading shotgun that has the appearance of a beefy AR-15 rifle. AR-15 fans will find the KRX shotgun easy to adjust to, as the safety selector, trigger, magazine release, and bolt stop will be familiar. The detachable five-round magazine is easily changed. This familiarity can be important for families preparing for self-defense and emergencies together with both rifles and shotguns, as it keeps training simple.

While handling the shotgun is different than handling an AR-15 rifle due to the weight and size of the shotgun (the rifle is both lighter and smaller), the KRX offers the same manual of arms as the rifle. There is a lot of plastic in this shotgun, and it isn't all hard polymer. This is a weight-saving measure.

I was only able to test a few shells of full-power buckshot, which of course won't tell the story for longevity and reliability, but the KRX seems to have promise.

SRM ARMS MODEL 1216

The SRM 1216 is among the most interesting shotguns to come along in some time. Similar in concept to the Kel-Tec KSG, it solves many capacity issues (including unwieldy and unbalanced shotguns with extended magazine tubes), with four four-round magazines while remaining a manually oper-ated pump-action shotgun. Unlike the KSG, the SRM 1216 features *rotating* magazine tubes. After the shotgun fires its first four shells, the bolt holds open. The shooter then rotates the next magazine tube into place to fire four more shells—but this is still faster than reloading a pump-action shotgun.

The SRM 1216 is a unique shotgun.

Available in several finishes, the SRM Arms 1216 is garnering a lot of attention.

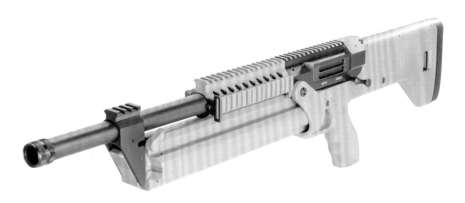

The SRM 1216 deserves an extensive training period before adoption for personal defense.

CHAPTER 11

RIOT SHOTGUNS, TACTICAL SHOTGUNS, AND SPECIALTY AMMUNITION

THE RIOT SHOTGUN

The pump-action 12 gauge with open Cylinder choke and 18-inch barrel, commonly referred to as a "riot shotgun," just may be the best all-around personal-defense firearm in the world. The 18-inch barrel configuration is compact enough for any foreseeable need. It handles quickly and swings from one target to the another rapidly in trained hands. It is easier manage than a full-length sporting shotgun, easier to keep at ready in a vehicle, and easily mounted in a secure shotgun mount inside a police cruiser or ranch vehicle. You may even mount the shotgun at home in the new Hornady wall safe configuration, a great product at a fair price and one that grants fast access to the firearm. The fixed Cylinder choke throws a wide pattern at distance, but for close-quarters defensive work, the pattern is sufficiently tight, though it will be a more open pattern at close range than the tactical shotgun equipped with a tighter screw-in choke.

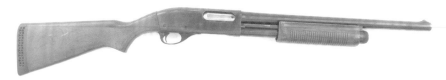

The Remington 870 is the archetypal riot gun.

There are several other traits that set the riot gun apart from other shotguns. There are shotguns in the riot format available in .410 and 20-gauge but the typical bead-sighted short-barreled gun is a 12-gauge. The riot shotgun will not have the magazine plugged for hunting. Magazine plugs, which are removable, are a legal requirement for bird hunting in several states. Inserted at the top of the magazine tube, they reduce the magazine capacity to two shells. Not only will a riot gun lack a magazine plug, extended tubes that increase magazine capacity to five to eight shells can be added. That's a lot of firepower and a sufficient reserve for many foreseeable emergencies.

The modern riot gun is as likely to have a synthetic stock as a traditional wood stock. The wood set, however, is the oldest riot gun setup and remains the most popular. One setup once more popular than it is now was the folding stock for the Remington 870. Used by many stakeout squads, the stocks made the shotgun easier to transport. The stock folded out to allow comfortable shoulder shooting, but when folded over the top of the shotgun gave the shooter a cruiser-type shotgun with a pistol grip.

It is interesting that the folding stock shotgun was readily available prior to 1900. The Burgess shotgun, for instance, was a true folder offered

The riot gun excels in tight quarters.

The Hornady wall safe is the ideal answer for keeping a shotgun at the ready but safe from unauthorized hands.

with a special leather holster for carrying under a suit coat! Prior to this, western bad guys and lawmen alike sometimes used short-barreled shotguns carried under the coat. These shotguns were balanced to hang muzzle down and sometimes had a stud in the pistol grip that aided carry.

These are the ancestors of the modern cruiser-type shotgun. The modern iterations are light and short

When one is backed into a corner, the riot gun is a great defensive weapon.

and quickly brought into action. Their downsides are that they are less controllable in rapid fire than standard-length shotguns, and a fold-over stock usually obscures the shotgun's sights, making for compromised aiming.

In my opinion, and as I have stated frequently in this book, the great efficiency of the riot gun for short-range anti-personnel work relies on the effectiveness of the 00 Buckshot load. Eight or nine 00 pellets can cause terrible and lethal damage at short range. Buckshot is effective for personal defense, depending upon the choke and the load, to about 20 yards, with 15 yards the ideal range.

While I prefer that 00 Buckshot load, there are contending viewpoints on the best load for self-defense with the riot gun. I have mentioned that the Hornady No. 4 Buckshot in the Varmint Express line originally gave me pause, but it turns out this load trades in a larger pellet size for sure hit probability and a dense pattern. I have tested it in my personal Remington 870 riot gun and it offered good penetration and a dense cloud of destruction. There is nothing wrong with updating an old tool with modern munitions, and those who praise No. 4 may have a point.

This old police shotgun has many years left in it.

If you wish to experiment with a load that is not the standard 00 Buckshot in your personal-defense shotgun, you should carefully pattern each choice before making the change. When choosing your combat load, remember that it is a large number of shot pellets striking the adversary instantly that effectively stops the aggression. Yes, you can go to smaller shot and get more hits, but then the question becomes, will those pellets hit hard enough and penetrate enough to stop the aggressor?

In my personal research, I keep coming back to buckshot as the answer, and 00 Buckshot seems the best all-around choice; for in-the-home personal defense, where you might worry about over-penetration and penetration through walls, No. 4 Buckshot makes a good alternative. There are loads such as the Winchester PDX1 that use both buckshot and a slug. I have found these loads to be effective and so offer yet another option.

Riot guns handle well during fast-moving drills thanks to their compact size.

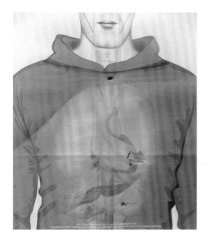

Riot guns may be used with the most modern loads. This is the pattern from a Winchester PDX1 buck-and-ball load at 20 yards.

Quickly loading the shotgun and keeping it in action is accomplished with practice.

THE TACTICAL SHOTGUN

When the shotgun is considered an all-around, go-anywhere, do-anything firearm for personal defense, the true riot gun with its 18-inch barrel and bead front sight isn't as effective as the tactical shotgun. The line between the riot gun and the tactical shotgun is thin sometimes, but the tactical shotgun has features the riot gun does not, such as a heat shield on the barrel for use when the barrel heats up after firing multiple shells very quickly. The tactical shotgun will also be fitted with open rifle sights, aperture sights, or the superior ghost ring sights. It may also be fitted with a red-dot scope or other optic, especially when long-range slug use is anticipated.

The basic riot gun may be updated with sensible upgrades such as the Adaptive Tactical stock and fore-end.

Keeping the Mossberg 500 tactical shotgun in action isn't difficult for those who practice diligently.

A short stroke of the slide and the pump-action riot gun is ready for another shot.

The Tactical Shotgun at Distance?

On the subject of long range, the 12-gauge shotgun with proper chokes is effective on clay birds, live birds, predators, and large game well past 25 yards, something not always realized by those who shoot shotguns intended for personal defense. Yes, longer barrels are better for such chores, but the tactical shotgun equipped with the right choke can also get the job done.

Larger game can be had at distance with a tactical shotgun as well. My uncles, for instance, have killed a lot of deer with shotguns, and they attested that buckshot has plenty of penetration at distance. Their deer were all killed within 100 yards, though the great majority at less than 50 yards. My Uncle Arden told me that, on occasion, he had skinned a buck that was killed by a lucky one or two pellets. I wouldn't want to bet that pellet or two against an aggressor armed with a rifle or even most handguns, but you can see where an accurate tactical gun loaded with slugs might do the trick.

The deer hunter using buckshot usually depends upon at least five buckshot pellet hits for a sure kill. A noted authority on personal-defense tells me that his research indicates that three hits are needed with 00 Buckshot in order to provide an effective wound and incapacitate an aggressor. Either way, if you want to be effective at distance with a tactical shotgun, you simply have to practice at extended distances to both know and have confidence in your gun, choke, and load (and any add-ons such as red-dot optics or scopes), as well as your ability to connect with your target.

SPECIAL AMMUNITIONS

Riot shotguns have a role in modern times not envisioned by their original inventors. They are, for instance, a great device for launching special munitions. I have had a number of good friends who performed security and law enforcement duties at airports, and they tell me the threat of birds causing aircraft to crash is real (recall the film *Miracle on the Hudson*). The task of clearing birds from the runway is an important one. Those friends tell me

The Mossberg 500 is a great shotgun that gives trained users every advantage. Note this version's extended magazine tube and heat shield.

Hornady Critical Defense buckshot is a super all-around defensive load for riot guns.

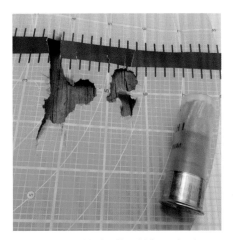

Slug accuracy with the Fiocchi Aero slug is often excellent to 15 yards with bead-sighted riot guns.

The Remington Express riot gun was a favorite for accuracy and smoothness of operation among testers for this book.

that shotgun-launched "bird bombs" are highly effective for frightening birds off runways and out of harm's way.

Less-lethal devices fired from the shotgun have seen much use in civil defense and police work. The bean-bag round, technically known as the "flexible baton round," is one such device. Tear gas rounds and the trade-marked Ferret projectiles (frangible munitions that have a chemical component to them and are used to penetrate barricades in order to disperse their chemical agent, thus "ferreting out" a hostage taker or other such adversary), are others.

Using the shotgun as a delivery device for those munitions categorized as "non-lethal" must be carefully considered (and not all non-lethal options are available to non-law enforcement persons). If any of these non-lethal choices are available to you, you must designate one specific firearm to be used *only* with those non-lethal munitions. In law enforcement and other tactical training circles, that firearm often wears a brightly colored stock totally different than other firearms in the arsenal, so that it is never mistaken for being loaded with traditional ammunition. This prevents miscues and tragedy from occurring.

Lightfield's Double Ball Non-Lethal Round

One non-lethal munition I've found may have some utility for home-owners is Lightfield's Home Defender 20-gauge Double Ball load. Intended for close-range defensive use, the load is designed to deliver a painful warning shot. With this ammunition, those who wish to defend themselves but cannot take the mental step of using lethal force can control their personal space with greater confidence. Another benefit, this load also provides a greater margin of safety to innocent persons nearby or in adjoining rooms.

The Home Defender 20-Gauge Double Ball round sends out twin .60-caliber balls that have high velocity but relatively low mass. The available kinetic energy is shed quickly over distance. Penetration of the body is possible at close range, and some level of injury should be expected. Though that can mean death—all munitions categorized as "non-lethal" carry the possibility of death—the generally expected result would range from painful welts and bruising to a blood-letting injury. Results can vary based on the weapon used, distance to target, clothing, body weight, and the anatomy hit. Shots to the lower body, legs, and arms are less likely to cause serious injury, while impacts to the head, neck, spine, and upper chest are more likely to be serious. Shots to parts of the body with large muscle groups, soft tissue, and those covered by clothing will have a lesser likelihood of penetrating.

The Wilson Combat Tactical model is far more advanced than a simple riot gun.

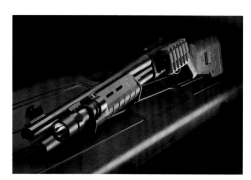

This Nighthawk custom shotgun offers a formidable upgrade to the run-of-the-mill riot gun.

Note the Surefire fore-end of this Nighthawk Custom shotgun.

Hornady TAP-FPD shotgun loads are ideal for service and home-defense use in the riot gun.

Rubber buckshot and tear gas rounds are often used in police and military shotguns. The bean-bag round is a bag filled with dense lead, fired as an intact unit, that is used to knock a person off their feet. Those engaged in psychotic behavior or threatening suicide but unarmed have frequently been temporarily incapacitated and rescued thanks to this type of projectile.

Another interesting use for the tactical shotgun is as a door-breaching device. Door breaching is often by both the military and police, though it does have application in emergency situations. For example, in the event that a catastrophic event to the nation has happened, the population has been decimated, and you are searching for food and other supplies, you might have to breach an abandoned building or store and access its goods to survive. Or you might have to rescue a loved one in likewise dire circumstances, say because of a building collapse in an earthquake or tornado.

The door-breaching shotgun is used to shatter hinges (and sometimes the main lock), thus providing a way to easily take down the door. The shotguns used in this role are typically very short-barreled and equipped with a serrated device on the muzzle that is placed against the lock or hinge to prevent slipping. This device adds to safety when firing the specialty door-breaching round. That specialty round is designed to expend all of its force on the door and not pose a threat to anyone on the other side.

Hornady developed the American Gunner slug for use in riot and tactical shotguns. This is a formidable loading.

Remington's tactical version of the 870 shotgun is a fine all-around fighting shotgun.

This is a military-issue, door-breaching shotgun based on the Remington 870.

CHAPTER 12

CUSTOM AND MODIFIED SHOTGUNS

The custom shotgun may be the ultimate expression of a shooter's wishes. The shotgun is fired largely by fit and feel (as opposed to aiming a rifle, a more deliberate method of shooting), so the shotgun is often modified to give a shooter a better "mesh" with their shotgun.

Wilson Combat's Border Patrol shotgun is at the top of the heap in custom grade firepower.

Customizations come in many shapes and forms. If we also manage to improve recoil control, that can be accomplished with recoil pads and mercury suppressors inserted in the buttstock. Sometimes we like to make the shotgun more compact, and changing the barrel and stock of a sporting shotgun to accomplish that goal can make it suitable for home- or area-defense. Fit can be customized through trimming, adding onto, or otherwise reshaping the buttstock's drop, comb, pitch, and cast. Custom stocks and fore-ends, AR-15-type stocks, chokes, porting, and back-boring, not to mention the addition of scopes, sights, and lights, are all custom measures that can benefit the all-around personal-defense shotgun. Let's look at some of this modern technology.

Magpul's SGA stock provides excellent fit and good combat utility for a wide variety of body sizes.

BACK-BORING

Back-boring isn't always well understood, but it is one relatively inexpensive customization that will benefit every shotgunner. Back-boring is simply opening the diameter of the shotgun barrel from the area just ahead of the chamber to the area just behind the choke. Also called "over-boring," this slight widening of the original gauge diameter is done via a lathe and a special custom reamer.

Back-boring was once a form of making or changing the effect of a choke for the shotgun, wherein the majority of the barrel was opened up a bit, but the choke end near the muzzle left at its original diameter. The practice of back-boring has many benefits, including lowering barrel pressure and enhancing patterns and choke performance. By widening the barrel gauge slightly, the wad cup containing the shot experiences less friction as it travels down the barrel. That means there's less compression on the shot itself and, therefore, reduced pellet deformation; deformed pellets tend not to fly with the regularity of their perfectly round cousins. Yes, a choke tighter than the barrel will compress the load, but that choke is only in the last inch or few inches of your barrel, so the compression is momentary compared to the time the load spends traveling down the rest of the barrel.

Remember, shot doesn't leave the barrel all at once in a flat plane. Shot pellets are stacked inside the shotshell hull and cup, so those at the top of the load and cup exit the barrel first, followed by those behind in what is called a "string." But it's not a straight-line string of one pellet after another. Shot exiting the barrel quickly does so in a column or cone, with the pellets spreading out the further they travel. Shoot a load—buckshot or birdshot, doesn't matter—at a patterning target set at five yards. Do the same at 10 yards, 15 yards, 25 yards, 30 yards, and 40 yards, and the "cone" will be apparent.

Both fixed chokes and modern screw-in choke tube performance may be improved by having the barrel back-bored. When the barrel is made larger in its internal dimensions but the pressure of the shell itself remains the same, you are in effect lowering the pressure of the shell. The shotgun shell's efficiency is therefore affected and you will effectively widen the shot column (top to bottom and side to side). At the same time, the length of the column (front to back) is shortened. This means all the pellets will arrive at their intended target faster. This is a desirable thing.

Back-bored barrels are more and more common on today's shotguns, especially those specifically designed for the clay target sports. Any modern barrel in good condition can be back-bored by a qualified gunsmith.

PORTING

Originally thought to reduce recoil, in my opinion, barrel porting has a negligible to non-existent effect on this. What porting the barrel (or extended screw-in choke tubes) does do is decrease muzzle rise. (Unfortunately, it also increases muzzle blast, often to ear-splitting levels.) That muzzle rise control is beneficial for clay bird competitors, but on a short-barreled home-defense gun, you'd likely not see an improvement (and the muzzle blast would be even worse than on a long-barreled sporting shotgun). In any case, I would avoid shotgun barrel porting. It can be a benefit on long choke tubes intended to aid the launching door breaching ammunition, but I think that those who are concerned with recoil would be better served by fitting a credible recoil pad to their shotgun.

TRIGGER WORK

Custom trigger action work on the shotgun should be approached with caution and should only be done by a qualified gunsmith. A trigger action must be safe above all else. A heavy trigger may be managed in the field, and even beneficial in times of high stress.

For long-range accuracy with slugs (and even some target and hunting applications), it is true that the 7½-pound trigger doesn't lend itself well to accuracy; a trigger that requires too much pressure to break can cause the shooter to pull the firearm off-target as the muscles in the hand tighten their grip in response to the increased leverage applied by the trigger finger. Thankfully, quite a few factory shotguns come with excellent triggers these days. For a slug gun, a trigger set to three to four pounds is ideal.

Double-barrel double triggers are often composed of a heavier forward trigger and a lighter rear trigger, when the opposite would be more beneficial. I've not found many gunsmiths capable of working on double-barrel triggers, so you may have to really do some research to find one if you think your shotgun would see improvement with this work.

Before you jump on a trigger job, consult a trigger-pull gauge. The RCBS trigger-pull gauge from Brownells.com will dispense with guesswork. Why? Because the problem you perceive as a too heavy trigger may actually be the stock's length of pull. Length of pull, generically, is the distance from the end of the stock to the flat curve of the trigger. You may be shooting too soon, flinching, or laying the trigger finger unevenly across the trigger because the trigger is too far to the rear or too far away for proper leverage. More on stocks in a bit.

PISTOL GRIPS

A few weeks ago, a friend purchased a Mossberg Cruiser shotgun with a pistol-grip stock. It looked cool, but, more important, it was easily stashed behind the rear seat of the man's Ford pickup. The problem came at the firing range. Its pistol grip gave new meaning to the term "wrist-snapping recoil."

With this shotgun, my friend was quickly introduced to flinch. Firing twenty full-power buckshot loads in the 12-gauge didn't help, and the following morning was spent soaking the wrist in Epsom salts.

The pistol-grip shotgun is okay for entry team use in crowded areas, and it's ideal for keeping handy in fishing trawlers to take out flipping, gnashing sharks brought in with the more mundane catches. As an all-around personal-defense shotgun, though, I think there are better choices. Harder to handle than a stocked shotgun, especially in a 12-gauge, this wouldn't be my first choice for an inexperienced shooter.

ADJUSTABLE STOCKS

If you find the pistol-gripped shotgun isn't your best all-around defensive shotgun, then you'll need one with a full-length stock. Stock lengths for shotguns tend to fall into two categories. The first has a length of pull usually in the 14½-inch range and is designed for the "average male;" in the US that male is generally about 5'9" to 5'10" and somewhere about 196 pounds. The second category of shotguns are often branded as "youth" or "ladies" shotguns. These have a length of pull ranging from 12½ to 13½ inches and are designed to "fit youth and smaller-statured adults;" the "average" US female is pegged somewhere around the 5'4" and 166-pound range.

"Average" was in quotes in that last paragraph because you can imagine how many people it takes to come up with that number (there are about 323 million people in the US), just as it takes little imagination to realize that we humans come in hundreds of shapes and sizes. Additionally, those shapes and sizes are affected by ethnicity and age. So, take the average for what it is—just that, an average—and then realize that a shotgun straight from the factory doesn't really fit much, if anyone, perfectly well, and many badly.

The solution is the adjustable stock. Some stocks are mildly adjustable, coming with a set of spacers that are inserted or subtracted from the juncture where the buttstock joins the receiver, or sometimes between the recoil pad and the end of the buttstock. Others have an adjustable comb, which can be raised, lowered, or moved a bit side to side. One adjustable recoil pad I've seen can be offset at the rear of the buttstock to the user's preference, thereby adjusting, without altering the actual stock at all, the cast, pitch, toe, and drop of the gun. Collectively, those four terms describe how straight up and down the shotgun is to the shooter's eye (you don't want a gun tilted off to one side or the other when it's shouldered), as well as how parallel the barrel is in line underneath the eye (i.e., the shooter is sighting flatly down the rib or barrel topline, rather than sighting up a ramp-like plane or looking down one side of the barrel or the other), when the gun is shouldered.

Many of these fit fixes are applied to shotguns intended for competition, and many branded for youths have the shims so that the gun can grow with the youth shooter. Wood-stocked shotguns can also be physically cut to length and even subjected to "bending" by specialized gunsmiths. "Bending" is what you imagine it is—bending the stock via a gradual process of heat-treating, blocks, and vises to achieve personally perfect cast, pitch, drop, and toe.

While the above can be a remedy for a poor-fitting wood stock, alteration options for synthetic stocks are fewer. Trimming a stock and installing a new recoil pad isn't nearly as easy as it is with a wood stock, and adjustable combs are few and far between on straight-from-the-factory, synthetic-stocked shotguns of traditional stock designs. What to do? Replace the stock.

I like the Magpul SGA stock. Available for Mossberg 500s and Remington 870s, this stock quickly solved the sore wrist for my friend with the pistol grip Mossberg 500. I put one on my personal Mossberg 500 as well. The greatest single advantage of this stock—and there are many—is its geometry.

I found its grip angle to be ideal for rapid handling. The stock has a unique turn that keeps the wrist properly slanted for excellent control. The stock comes with four spacers that allow modification to the length of pull, and you do not have to remove the buttpad to change the length of pull. I have on hand a youth model Mossberg 500 and a standard stocked version. The shorter SGA stock configuration is in between the two and works great for my use. On my full-size 500, I installed the SGA in its shortest configuration for easy storage and rapid deployment.

This is some of the hardware used to adjust the Magpul SGA stock.

There are other worthwhile features to the SGA. The stock offers right- or left-hand sling attachment. The stock itself isn't difficult to install, is more rigid than

Note the excellent stippling of the SGA stock.

the AR-15-type stock, and is affordable in the realm of high-quality gear. Its hard polymer material is the same that Magpul uses in all of its well-regarded rifle parts. This means durability under harsh conditions.

The full range of length-of-pull adjustments were had in ½-inch increments from its shortest length of 12½ inches to its longest of 14½ inches. The buttpad is designed to help soften recoil, and the gripping area is suitably roughened for good adhesion. Finally, there are optional cheek risers for those wishing to use red dot scopes or other optical sighting equipment.

A modern AR-15-type stock, such as the one from Adaptive Tactical, is another option for tactical shotguns. If you fit this kind of stock to a shotgun and you also own an AR-15-type rifle, you have the commonality of controls. This can be very beneficial when transitioning from one firearm to another and for

The Magpul SGA offers a wide range of adjustment.

family members who may be sharing firearms, as this eliminates some of the learning curve between the two. Of course, these stocks offer a great deal of fit flexibility, again ideal when more than one person may need to utilize the firearm, for adjusting to various outerwear such as a tactical vest, and because in their shortest, most collapsed setting these stocks improve the ability to store or transport the shotgun.

FACTORY CUSTOM

One of the better shotguns I have handled is the Wilson Combat adaptation of the Remington 870 shotgun, and it's one that proves the adage "You get what you pay for." Taking a proven fight-stopping shotgun and modifying it to custom status isn't easy, but Wilson Combat did it.

Smooth in operation and highly tuned, the Wilson Combat shotgun is well worth its price.

It began with proven baselines from the former Scattergun Technologies Company it purchased and the Remington Model 870. Choosing the 870 shotgun wasn't done lightly. This shotgun has been proven in combat the world over. Accessories, barrels, and spare parts are plentiful; in my entire

The Wilson Combat shell carrier, aperture sights, and adjustable stock are hallmarks of the modern tactical shotgun.

The combination of features on the Wilson Combat tactical shotgun makes for an ideal tactical-grade combat shotgun.

shooting life, I have needed exactly one trigger return spring for the 870 shotgun. Few would argue that the Remington 870 is the standard against which all other pump-action shotguns are judged.

That doesn't mean there isn't room for improvement. Wilson offers four custom models: The Border Patrol, CQB, Professional,

The Wilson Combat tactical shotgun is loaded up and ready for action.

and Standard. There's also a Less Lethal variant that, while it will fire any 12-gauge ammunition, can be instantly identified as being loaded with bean-bag or rubber-shot ammunition by its unique, bright-orange stock (helpful in riots or other complex scenarios where many defenders or law enforcement personnel are involved and less-lethal remedies may be deployed before others). The following will focus on the Standard model.

Wilson's Standard 870 features a Cylinder choke in a barrel that measures a tactically appropriate 18½ inches. Next, the shotgun wears a matte finish similar to parkerizing. This is a big deal for me. Having seen many Remington 870s develop corrosion from wear on the long flats and bevels of the receiver and other high-use areas, the Wilson Combat Armor-Tuff finish is a welcome addition.

A good fighting shotgun, especially one for launching special munitions or for slug use, needs sights that are a step above and beyond the simple front bead. Wilson Combat offers a Trak-Lock ghost ring rear sight. The front sight is a ramped type with a tritium insert. The addition of a luminous iron sight is a good touch, as it provides excellent utility in low light. Ghost ring sights on their own are excellent additions, as they provide a high-profile aiming point the eye picks up

Note the attention to detail and excellent fit and finish of the Wilson Combat modified 870.

quickly. For those who will be using slugs at longer range, the fully adjustable rear sight is appreciated. Both elevation and windage adjustments are positive. The front sight is solidly attached. These sights give a trained user the ability to home shotgun slugs to at least 50 yards with a high degree of accuracy.

Wilson Combat's fiber optic front sight is highly visible in low-light conditions.

Sights are good, but so is target identification. The Standard model shotgun is equipped with a fore-end integrating a 200- to 600-lumen Surefire tactical light. This is a great upgrade for a combat shotgun and I like this addition very much. The Standard also utilizes a special extended safety button. I have never experienced any difficulty with the standard Remington 870 safety, but the extended safety doesn't hurt anything and may be an advantage with gloved hands.

Wilson Combat shotguns are intended for 24-hour duty in all light and environmental conditions.

The shotgun is supplied with a six-round extended magazine tube, an improvement over the standard Remington 870 and its four-shell tube. A receiver-mounted sidesaddle shell carrier adds another four to six rounds.

This shotgun does have a stock shorter than average, in order to account for the use of body armor. I like this stock, and the recoil pad seems adequate for the chore at hand. As of this writing, the Standard Model lists for $1,540 and is the least expensive of Wilson's several custom shotguns. It is smooth in operation and definitely more pleasurable to shoot than standard rack-grade shotguns.

No space is wasted. Note the firing handle with its battery-pack compartment.

Robar (robarguns.com) is another company that upgrades the Remington 870 and Mossberg shotguns. Working with either model, the barrel is re-crowned and a VanComp ghost ring sight added. The barrel is back-bored and the forcing cone lengthened. The action is improved in a process that involves polishing the interface between the action bars and the operating fore-end. The result is a smoother action that's less likely to short cycle. A large safety button is also installed, a popular option I do not necessarily need, but one handy if shooting with gloves. Robar's trigger job, on the other hand, I think is a worthwhile upgrade.

Robar's package also includes a magazine tube extension with a clamp and sling stud. A small but important touch for tactical shotguns is the high-visibility magazine follower. I like the one on my Remington 870, as it gives a visual indication you have run dry. Other Robar modifications include a Pachmayr Decelerator recoil pad that reduces the factory length of pull by one inch. The Robar non-slip texture is added to the pistol grip and fore-end, as is a side-saddle shell holder. Finally, a sling swivel

The Surefire combat light melds nicely into the Wilson Combat fore-end.

An extended magazine and Surefire fore-end enhance the usability of the basic 870.

The Surefire tactical fore-end with combat light is a smart addition to the Wilson Combat Standard model setup.

In the long run, the Wilson Combat shotgun with its finely finished parts and improvements is more likely than a stock shotgun to withstand the rigors of hard use and training.

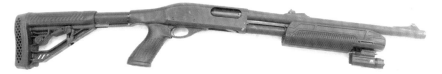

This old Remington 870 has been given a new and more useful role with the addition of Adaptive Tactical hardware.

and stud are installed on the buttstock. This is a great all-around package for dedicated tactical shotgunners.

The author prefers the Adaptive Tactical stock among M4 variations.

I have been reluctant to fit after-market parts to my firearms for risk of losing both familiarized handling and reliability. Among the companies I trust is Adaptive Tactical, which offers a number of excellent products. One of those is the AR-15 stock I talked about earlier. Another is the Sidewinder Venom shotgun magazine conversion kit that lets your pump-action shotgun accept a detachable box magazine in five- and 10-round configurations. The conversion is available for the Remington 870 and Mossberg 500, 88 (Maverick), and 590 shotguns.

The Venom conversion kit includes an adjustable length-of-pull M4-style stock with pistol grip and Adaptive Tactical's Wraptor fore-end. This fore-end includes a heat shield and three Picatinny rails for accessory mounting. Although it is designed for owner installation, I'll tell you that you should take your shotgun and the kit to a qualified gunsmith and pay for the fitting. The cost is reasonable and worth having someone else do work.

You will have to spend the bucks for spare magazines to take the full advantage of this conversion, if course, but they hold the 2¾-inch shells. The five-round magazine is a box magazine, while the 10-round is available both in box and in rotary drum configurations.

There are cautions with the Adaptive Tactical Sidewinder Venom setup. One is the expense, but then this is new and innovative technology. The shotgun also handles much differently from the pump-action shotgun in its original configuration. The tradeoff is that the higher magazine capacity and detachable magazines give a decided advantage in trained hands.

The Adaptive Tactical kit offers advanced utility, especially with the 10-round magazines.

I may not be completely sold on the Venom magazine conversion, but then it took me many years to investigate the effectiveness of the Kel-Tec KSG. (I like my older guns, what can I say?) I am, however, completely

The Adaptive Tactical fore-end allows mounting of a combat light.

convinced of the utility of the EX Performance stock and fore-end, also by Adaptive Tactical.

Some time ago I was asked to test this combination. I chose a twenty-year-old Remington 870 Police Magnum shotgun with which to do that. This rifle-sighted shotgun has faithfully stuck by my side and served as the tester for any number of munitions. It has endured rough treatment and demonstrated excellent utility.

The EX Performance fore-end is a high-impact polymer piece featuring a two-inch Picatinny rail hidden under a removable nose cap. With the cover removed, the rail is well suited to fitting lights or lasers. The fore-end is a bit longer than the Remington original.

The EX Performance buttstock features a rapid-adjust lever for instant length-of-pull alterations. The recoil pad is both non-slip and vented. I like the buttstock's M4 configuration, and while I still deploy conventional stocks,

I intend to keep the Remington 870 fitted with this Adaptive Tactical stock and fore-end ready in the truck. If you need a quality modern stock that makes your shotgun (Remington 870 and Mossberg 500, 88 (Maverick), and 590 shotguns) suitable for tactical use, one that's comfortable to shoot with slug loads and mimics the fit and feel of the AR-15 stock, the Adaptive Tactical combination is a smart choice.

As of this writing, the Adaptive Tactical EX Performance kit has been mounted on my 870 shotgun for over a year. I appreciate the ruggedness and engineering of this set-up. After an acclimation period, I found that quick and accurate hits at long range were improved with this setup.

REFINISHING OPTIONS

Most shotguns are supplied with a blue finish that seems best suited for the shooter who will return home from the hunting field and spend time oiling the finish to prevent corrosion. High-polished blue finishes can wear quickly. With hard use, the matte blue finish on affordable shotguns deteriorates even faster.

A durable finish is desirable from a longevity standpoint—the rusted gun gets you nowhere. Parkerizing is an alternative that improves upon the high-polish and standard matte bluing finishes, but there are other better finishes available. One of these is Robar's NP3 finish, a superior type of electroless nickel. I have used this finish on stainless steel, steel, and aluminum with excellent results. Many agencies use this finish on their handguns and shotguns, and this is also a popular finish for bolt carriers, which show their wear easily. NP3 has also been used on the space station! The biggest advantage of NP3 is a co-deposit of sub-micron PTFE or polytetrafluoroethylene

This image of the Robar refinishing job speaks for itself.

particles—Teflon. When Teflon is alloyed with electroless nickel, you have a tremendously durable finish. Microscopic analysis shows that NP3 covers the substrate metal, while PTFE is integrated into the finish.

There are many benefits claimed for NP3. Primary is that it permits firing for longer periods of time between cleaning. Dirt, powder, and other residues simply have nothing to which they can cling. Even when I do clean my guns with an NP3 finish, the effort required to clean them is much less than with firearms not so treated.

The NP3 compound also provides excellent lubricity. Indeed, the finish is self-lubricating and does not require additional lubrication on long bearing surfaces.

Eccentric wear is what causes parts to need to be replaced. That's another benefit of NP3, as friction is limited. The finish may also be applied to the smallest parts, including action parts, and NP3 coating results in a smoother action. The finish itself is a dull gray, non-reflective satin finish. It is both attractive and business-like. While the NP3 finish, like any other, may be damaged by dropping or other blunt impact, when the finish is damaged there seems little chance of corrosion getting a foothold. NP3 has a lifetime warranty.

NP3 Plus is another finish developed by Robar. I have handled and fired but one example with NP3 Plus finish, but the new development seems ideal for marine use. I have seen many Marine shotguns with stainless or nickel parts, and I have to tell you that their finishes will corrode. Stainless steel is just that—stain-less—and will pit like mad. Robar's testing of the NP3 Plus shows it can withstand a salt spray test, the standard of the industry, with 1,000 hours of exposure with only one mil (.001-inch) of NP3 Plus coverage. That is impressive. In common with NP3, NP3 Plus features the PTFE component that is deposited throughout the coating.

Robar offers a number of dark finishes that are resistant to corrosion and which offer excellent results when applied to steel and alloy steels, including stainless. A little history: Before they were blue, firearms were supplied in the brown. Browning and cold-bluing are similar in process, and both are simply a process for finishing metal using oxidation, making them more corrosion resistant. A matte black finish is produced via chemical reaction with the trace elements in steel in order to form a black oxide coating.

For those who like the aesthetics of these finishes but wish for something hardier, Robar's process does not chip, flake, peel, or create any change in critical dimensions. The company's Roguard finish meets every requirement for a military and police use. I like the Roguard appearance very much, particularly on the classic shotguns, though it is equally at home on any modern tactical shotgun.

CHAPTER 13

SHOTGUN SIGHTS AND OPTICS

SIGHT BASICS

There are three basic types of shotgun iron sight setups: The simple bead (either a single bead at the muzzle or the muzzle bead with a second mid-rib bead), aperture or ghost ring sights, and rifle sights. With optical sights, there are shotgun slug rifle scopes and red dot

The bead is attached to the barrel rib in a sporting shotgun.

These sights are found on the Hawk 82 shotgun. They are good examples of aperture sights.

When using aperture sights, the type that are tightened onto a rail should be checked often. These fell off the Tec-12 during a training session.

Among factory units, you cannot top the Benelli rear sight.

This rear sight from Wilson Combat is ideal for combat use.

optics (both tubular and reflex in design). The advantages of each are worth considering when evaluating a shotgun for home or personal defense.

Shotguns may be fired intuitively, by feel and handling, or they can be aimed like a rifle. A moving target demands fast action, swinging, and firing by feel. In shooting moving targets, the focus is also on the target, with the front bead in the periphery; reverse this to focus on the bead and you'll miss. Conversely, a stationary target at longer range demands strict use of the sights and deliberate aiming, with a focus on the front sight, while the rear sight (if there is one) and the target are blurred in soft focus. It is swinging to shoot where the target will be versus aiming to shoot where the target is. Target focus versus front sight focus. It is that simple.

Different sights accommodate these two distinctly different methods of hitting the target. As an example, we usually get our eye on the flying game first and then use the shotgun bead in the periphery to gauge when to pull the trigger so that the shot string strikes where that moving target is going to be. In personal defense, the bead is picked up in a fast flash sight picture as the muzzle is centered on the aggressor's center of mass. Rifle-type shotgun sights are used by picking up the front sight in focus while coordinating it to center within the gap in the rear sight for careful aiming. The ghost ring, a variation in the rifle sight, is brilliantly fast for the person who knows how to quickly shoulder the shotgun and get it into action. With this sight design, shoulder the shotgun and look through the rear aperture, the ghost ring. The rear sight fades from clarity as the eye centers and focuses on the front sight viewed through that aperture. Many tactical shotgun practitioners like ghost sights because the front post seems to center itself within that rear aperture, and this can favor rapid-paced buckshot and slug work.

With anything other than a single bead, knowledge of how your sights work in various circumstances is as important as the sight choice itself. Sights used quickly and at close range will rarely provide a perfect sight picture. Instead, you will get a "flash" sight picture and go to work with what you have; getting the front sight on the target quickly will usually suffice for a good hit with the shotgun. At longer effective

A simple bead front sight offers fast acquisition of the target in most situations at close range, but isn't ideal for long-range work.

shotgun range, longer usually beginning at 10 yards, you must slow down and concentrate on getting the sights properly aligned in order to produce a good hit. The shooter who uses his sights must have practiced with them often in order to remain calm and react quickly in an attack, remembering to use the sights instead of simply thrusting the shotgun to the shoulder and firing.

Note the wide range of adjustment of Benelli's tactical rear sight.

This Benelli system self-loader features rifle sights.

This is the back side of a Benelli rear sight.

The shrouded rear sight of the Benelli tactical shotgun is ideal for most uses.

Remington's Buck Special sight is useful for accurate slug work.

A good-quality front sight must complement the rear sight. This unit is found on a Benelli Nova tactical pump.

Remington's post front sight complements the Buck Special or riot gun rifle-type sights.

SHOTGUN RIBS

The rib is an important part of the shotgun and should be understood whether yours has one or not.

The rail or rib on a Mossberg 500.

The side-by-side was the first shotgun to employ a barrel rib. Initially merely fixing the barrels strongly together, ribs came to be utilized for aiming. But the broad sight—the rib and bead with a barrel on either side—was simply too large to be effective; those early ribs had their single bead buried in the trough between the two barrels. Shots for those unpracticed tended to go low. Eventually, a raised rib replaced the original. This was an improvement, because the rib and its bead, slightly elevated over the top of the barrels, was now more in line with the shooter's sightline to the target. Given a proper gun fit, connecting with flying game became easier (i.e., the angled accruement called the rib isn't for aiming and rifle-like accuracy, but is meant to lead the shooter's eye to the muzzle and the bead front sight, then to the target where the focus should be). Another advantage of the rib is that it keeps the barrels from vanishing under bright sunlight by disrupting the glare of a shiny bright-blue barrel otherwise unadorned.

Some ribs have dual beads, one mid-rib and one at the muzzle. Depending on the shotgun and the pitch of the rib, they are designed to be seen in the periphery as a figure-eight (the muzzle bead sitting directly on top of the mid-rib bead when the gun is shouldered and the head is on the stock) or to be in line and appear as one. This provides a reference to the shooter, letting them know that the gun is straight between the hands (i.e., it's not canted sideways) and shouldered so as send a centered shot (i.e., neither one too high nor too low).

A shotgun rib is a flat piece of metal running from the front of the receiver down the top length of the barrel to end at the muzzle. Flat ribs, also known as the straight rib, are most common. Some are designed to give the illusion of a longer barrel and a longer sight radius, which can be beneficial to connecting with targets at longer ranges. Ventilated ribs are used to diffuse radiant heat in shotguns intended for use in competition or hunting when many shells will be fired quickly. Ventilated ribs also offer aesthetic appeal and, in the case of some specialty competition trap guns, stepped to aid in connecting with targets thrown at long, specific distances.

Ribs aren't usually a consideration in combat shooting. The single-barrel shotgun in its earliest forms used but a simple front bead, and many if not most designed for self-defense still come equipped this way. (One thing to keep in mind when using

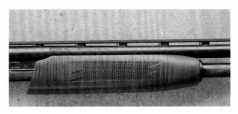

Mossberg offers excellent rails at a reasonable price.

a more sporting-oriented shotgun with a bead front sight and no rib is that you'll have a tendency to fire low at medium ranges when shooting slugs. Changing to a barrel with a rib can remedy this.) When you purchase a bead-only shotgun, one accessory you should consider adding is a Hi-Viz fiber optic sight. Especially with aging eyes, but for anyone who expects to be shooting in low-light situations, this can greatly aid accuracy.

SHOTGUN SCOPES

For improved slug accuracy, the shotgun may be fitted with a scope. Such a scope must be rugged and capable of taking a beating from shotgun recoil (which is different than rifle recoil).

TruGlo's 4X scope has become one of my preferences, after mounting it on one of the 870s for testing. The TruGlo scope outclassed my accuracy with the bead-only smoothbore Remington, and on a rifled slug gun it would have been terrific.

A majority of new-production semi-auto and pump-action receivers are drilled and tapped for mounting an optical sight. Some feature cantilever mounts that attach directly to the barrel, allowing the barrel to be removed and maintain zero when remounted.

The TruGlo shotgun scope is ideal for slug use.

TruGlo's affordable red dot sights offer excellent function.

RED DOT OPTICS

For most defensive needs, the bead front sight is king of the hill. But for slug use and when the shotgun is forced into rifle-type work, then some type of sight can be an advantage. Deer hunting and turkey hunting are among the field uses for which a quality electronic red dot optic is a great help. They provide a specific aiming reference point once properly sighted in, and the dot can be adjusted for intensity (and sometimes size), making these optics useful in a variety of lighting conditions. Today's red dot sights are also compact and add little to the bulk and weight of the shotgun, thus maintaining the gun's balance and fast handling. That also means they are good for personal defense.

I have mounted a red dot scope on my Kel-Tec KSG. The shotgun as delivered had no sighting equipment at all. I considered iron sights of the standard AR-15 variety, but decided to try the TruGlo red dot for this book—and after I mounted this sight and trained with it, there's nothing else I'll ever put on this particular shotgun. Why? In a situation of self-defense, when the distance for shooting is short, you are inevitably also short on time. For those

Red dot optics require practice, if you are to be effective with them. Use them in different lighting, from behind and around cover, and any other way that might replicate a worst-case situation you might find yourself in someday.

At long range, something more than a bead front sight is needed. Slug accuracy can be outstanding with proper iron sights.

who practice with them, the red dot sight provides an edge in speed (faster sight picture) and accuracy (put the dot on the target and connect). It can also extend your range.

Of all the ways to look down a shotgun barrel and connect with a distant target, I think that the red dot is the one that benefits defensive shooters the most. Too, they're a problem-solver for many with less than perfect vision.

I have suffered some loss of visual acuity with age. This means that I cannot maintain a perfect focus on a rifle-type front sight post (important when aiming the shotgun like a rifle at a static target). My eyes are not as fast to focus as they use to be, and while my unaided eyesight is good, it certainly isn't what it used to be. With the red dot scope, the focal point is in one spot and one spot only. No more trying to get my eyes to focus on the front sight and keeping that focus sharp.

My eyesight aside, I have trained quite a few shooters on the red dot scope. Those who have had a difficult time with other types of aiming devices or iron sights often groove into the red dot quickly. That's an edge when more than one person might need to use a particular firearm.

As great as they are, there is one shortcoming to the red dot you should be aware of: They are not infallible. Like every device that runs on batteries, that battery will run out at some point. And as sturdy as they are—and today's red dots are very durable—knock one too hard the wrong way and you're going to break it or otherwise render it useless. Today's red dot sights are compact and add little to the bulk and weight of the shotgun. Still, I'll keep a watch on my battery life and reap their many benefits. If the lights go out and I have to aim through the red dot glass, for instance, I am far from helpless with buckshot (obviously, the ability to precision shoot with slugs is gone in the dark).

When deploying a red dot, be certain that you practice regularly to master the optic's use. By doing so, you will be as fast at close range with the red dot as with a simple bead front sight, while also improving your long-range accuracy.

Red dot sights are better than ever, even some of the relatively inexpensive sights. If your life depends on the sights, though, go with the best quality you can afford. Bushnell, Burris, TruGlo, Leupold, and Nikon are names well worth their prices.

A subset of the red dot sight are found with the reflex and holographic sights. Doing away with tube of more traditional optics, these single-lens units weigh just ounces. If this is your choice in sighting aids, look for those with the lowest profile, so that a traditional or ghost ring rear sight and front sight may be "co-witnessed" with the red dot, meaning you can use one or the other, especially if one fails. You must also choose a sight that allows fast and sure close-quarter acquisition with both eyes open (the ability to *easily* keep both eyes open is actually one of the benefits of the reflex and holographic sights). The sight should have premium coated glass with a protected lens and parallax-free sight picture.

Red dot sights do allow you to do away with a front and rear sight their two planes of focus. With a red dot sight, you have just two things to focus on—the dot and where on the target you're holding that dot. With the fast-moving type of defensive shooting we practice with the shotgun, the red dot sight is especially well suited. Tactical use, home defense, and 3-Gun competition are among the uses the red dot suits well.

Meopta's MeoRed

One of my top optic choices for all-around use is the Meopta MeoRed, a lightweight and compact red dot sight. I have used Meopta optics for some time and find the quality and value excellent. The operator may move the red dot without blocking the iron sights of the shotgun with this unit. In other words, it easily co-witnesses. This is critical for self-defense work. When the battery or the sight fails—and it will fail at some point—you can stay in the fight by co-witnessing the gun's original sights.

The MeoRed sight uses aircraft-grade aluminum alloy construction. It is rated water- and shockproof. The MeoRed may be mounted on either a military standard 1913 Picatinny rail mount or a Docter mount, which is included with the MeoRed sight from the factory.

The Meopta MeoRed sight offers excellent utility for its price which, while not inexpensive, would be considered affordable by most.

When sighting in the MeoRed, note that there is lots of room for adjustment: 180 MOA windage and 120 MOA elevation. Play with these adjustments at the various distances you practice to get a thorough feel for where the dot is in relation to your hits.

Note the ease of adjustment thanks to the wide range of windage and elevation clicks on the MeoRed.

To operate the MeoRed, simply turn the control button on the left side of the sight body to the "On" position. This activates the red dot, which covers 3 MOA in its standard setting. The brightness level is adjustable; just choose what works best your particular conditions. As an example, I find that when working inside a training building to replicate a home-defense situation, a moderately bright dot works well in dim surroundings. When running the MeoRed in the daylight for practice, you'll likely need a brighter setting.

With any red dot sight, battery life is a concern, and some sights have longer life than others. The MeoRed uses a CR 2032 battery the company says is good for three hundred hours of continuous use. That is a credible amount of battery life that should serve most anyone's needs well.

Still, the question is always about how much battery is left. Few of us will use the red dot for three hundred continuous hours, but how often have any of us forgotten to turn off something that was battery operated when we were done using it? Meopta addresses this concern with a low-battery indicator. There's also an auto-off feature. If the function button isn't touched over a three-hour period, the sight simply turns itself off.

A door in the side compartment of the MeoRed allows easy battery exchange.

When it does come time to change the battery on the MeoRed, it's a fast and simple task and one that can be completed without taking the sight off the firearm. Locate the battery door on the right of the sight. The door is held on by two small screws (this prevents the door from popping open during recoil or otherwise accidentally being wedged open). Pop out the old battery, put in the new, and screw the door back on.

CHAPTER 14

TRAINING WITH YOUR SELF-DEFENSE SHOTGUN

The shotgun is at its best defending against threats that might be encountered at home or on the ranch. This could range from a coyote raiding a chicken coop to a criminal invading your home in the middle of the night. In the realm of emergency preparation, the shotgun's use might extend to protecting precious food and water supplies from vermin contamination or human theft, defending your shelter, and acquiring some much-needed protein through hunting.

Your body stance is critical to controlling the shotgun.

No matter the situation, you must have thought about how you will use the shotgun to address them and trained to be effective for each. Without the skills to properly and safely use your shotgun, you risk injuring yourself or other innocent bystanders. This chapter will address the issues of safety, tactics you should practice, and scenarios for which you should prepare. All the training, drills, and scenarios outlined in this chapter may be adapted to any shotgun action design (though each action will also have its individual accommodations that will need to be met).

SAFETY—FIRST, LAST, AND ALWAYS

Understanding safe firearms handling is paramount to responsible firearms ownership. It should be the first thing you think about before you pick up a gun, ever-present while you're handling them, and encompass your final review before storing them. The following seven rules must be followed every time you handle a firearm:

1. Treat every gun as if it's loaded, every time, all the time. Even when you have unloaded a firearm and verified there is no ammunition in it through a physical and visual inspection, you must still treat it as if it is loaded.
2. Always keep your firearm pointed in a safe direction.
3. Keep your finger off the trigger until you are ready to shoot.
4. Never point your firearm at something you do not wish to destroy.
5. Know your target and what lies beyond it.
6. Never handle a firearm while intoxicated.
7. Always wear eye and hearing protection on the practice range and where otherwise appropriate.

There's one more point of safety to consider, and that's how you store your firearms. Traditional thought tells you to store all firearms unloaded, locked away, and with ammo securely stored in a different location. That's great for a perfect world, but if you're about to encounter a life-or-death emergency, it's not likely practical.

That means many people will want to keep firearms loaded and close at hand. Many authorities on defense in the home also encourage staging weapons in various rooms so that you can immediately access to protection no matter where you are in your home when an invasion occurs. That may be smart, and it may work for some households, but you still have to guard against unauthorized access to those firearms and other weapons.

Unauthorized persons include burglars, children, friends who snoop through your home during a party, etc. You'll have to weigh the *availability* of the loaded firearm—how fast you can get it into action—against the possibility of unauthorized use.

This is an easier subject to tackle with handguns, with dozens of instant-access cypher and biometric combination safes available to them. Long guns don't have much available to them in that realm. So that leaves you with a multitude of action and trigger locks and firearm floor safes to consider. There are also furniture pieces designed to conceal long guns that appear as just another dresser or wardrobe—i.e., they aren't obvious like a traditional armored floor safe would be—and which can provide instant access to the right person.

The "right person" is key to any of this. You must *always* prevent children from accessing your firearms. That includes securing ammunition that goes in a particular firearm away from that firearm. Kids are curious—and that's how tragic accidents happen. Drunk houseguests happen too, and you certainly don't want your firearms stolen during a break-in and out on the street better arming the criminal element. Think, think hard, about how and where you store your firearms. Train, train hard, to remove them from secure storage and get them into action. You have just as much responsibility (if not more) for preventing unauthorized use of your firearms as you do employing a one for personal self-defense.

KNOW YOUR FIREARM

A lack of familiarity with any particular firearm is a safety issue, so take the time to thoroughly understand your firearm inside and out. When purchasing, ensure the salesperson has reviewed the mechanical safeties of the firearm and explained how the gun functions, how it should be loaded, and how it should be unloaded. Once home, reading the owner's manual will answer many common questions and instruct you on how to properly maintain your firearm.

I have spent years instructing others and prefer even the most novice shooter come to me with a basic knowledge of how their firearm functions. For you reading this, that may not be possible. If you have purchased or otherwise acquired a firearm and do not know how to operate it (including to verify its loaded or unloaded condition):

1. Take it to a knowledgeable firearms retailer and have them go over the gun with you. You *must* remember the seven firearms safety rules above when doing this, *especially* if you are unable to determine the firearm is unloaded before entering the store with it and asking for help. If you do not know whether the firearm is unloaded, you *must* tell the person behind the counter helping you. It can even be prudent to leave the firearm in your vehicle, ask the salesperson to come outside with you, and let them take it inside the store.

2. Arrange to meet with a firearms instructor and have them go over the gun with you. You *must* remember the seven firearms safety rules above when doing this, *especially* if you are unable to determine the firearm is unloaded before meeting the instructor. If you do not know whether the firearm is unloaded, you *must* tell the instructor before he or she begins working with you. It can even be prudent to leave the firearm in your vehicle, ask the instructor to go to your vehicle with you, and let them handle the gun to take it inside the store or onto the range.

While I'm betting the above is familiar information for most reading this book, it's good to remember that everyone had to start somewhere. Nobody was born knowing about firearms safety and shooting technique any more than they were born knowing how to drive or cook dinner. Too, there are millions of firearms out there, and it's a fair bet that even the most experienced shooters occasionally run across a firearm or action they don't know how to operate. Safety never takes time off. So, with the above covered, let's move on and assume you're familiar with the shotgun you've chosen for your emergency preparations, including loading and unloading and you have a feel for how it shoots.

Note: Every suggested form of practice or drill you'll read about in the following pages should be undertaken only on an established firearms range approved for the type of practice you intend to perform and with the proper berms and backstops in place. Always follow the range rules regarding hot ranges (live-fire occurring), cold ranges (cease fire commands), targets and target stands that can be used, what type of shotgun ammunition can be used, and what movements on the firing line are allowed. Be considerate of others on the range and clean up and remove your shot targets and expended hulls at the end of your shooting session. Above all else, remember the rules of firearms safety—first, last, and always.

FUNCTION TESTING

Before any live-fire practice session, you should perform a functionality test on your firearm.

To begin, point your unloaded firearm in a safe direction, keeping your finger off the trigger. Verify with your fingers and eyes that there is no ammunition in the chamber/s of a single-shot or double-barrel, nor in the magazine of a pump-action or semi-automatic. There should be no barrel obstruction/s.

Unless otherwise noted, from here forward the text will relate strictly to pump-actions and semi-automatics.

Manually manipulate the action:

1. For a semi-automatic, pull the bolt handle back until it locks in place. Depress the bolt release button and send the bolt home to close completely.
2. For a pump-action, manipulate the slide smoothly and positively to open and then close the bolt.

Load a round in the magazine. Be certain it is properly seated and that the shell properly catches and is retained within the magazine. Repeat the

When racking the pump-action shotgun, it is important to bring the operating rods completely to the rear with a positive motion.

action manipulation for your action type and then verify that the round has been loaded into the chamber by slightly opening up the action. Finish loading the magazine.

Unload your shotgun. You can do this by carefully and slowly manually cycling the action and allowing the shells coming from the magazine to roll out of the ejection port, rather than sliding them home to chamber. Another method will have you eject the loaded shell in the chamber, then turn the gun upside down and depress its cartridge stop, usually located on the right side of the receiver (now on your left since the gun is upside down), and removing each shell in the magazine until empty. This works for most semi-autos and pumps. Note, though, that each shotgun will have its operating controls and safeties in different places, and not all controls of similar purpose function alike, so be sure to consult the owner's manual for specific instructions on safely loading and unloading your particular shotgun.

Your functionality test is now complete, and you can proceed with live-fire practice.

THE COMBAT STANCE

Ideally, when in a firefight, you'll be taking your shots from behind cover. Ideally doesn't always happen. You may be going about your business, say

We have the 12-gauge shotgun on target and a shell making a trail in the humid air. The stance keeps the shotgun on target!

walking between your home and a barn or toolshed, when a bad situation quickly unfolds. Or maybe you have to quickly deploy your shotgun and get rid of that pesky coyote halfway into the chicken coop. Either way, you need to be balanced in a way that allows you to make accurate shots, handle the recoil, and has you prepared for movement.

Note the author is leaning into the shotgun to better absorb the recoil.

Your firing stance is one of the most important fundamentals of working effectively with a tactical shotgun in preparation for self-defense. In this stance, a fighting stance, your head is held erect, the strong-side (trigger) elbow is perpendicular to the ground, and the support arm parallel to the ground. Your legs will be positioned a bit wider than your shoulders, with the leg on the same side as your fore-end arm a little further ahead and supporting the greater portion of your body's weight. The knee on this forward leg should be bent slightly; the knee of the leg to the rear should not be locked. The stock should be pressed

Practice getting the shotgun into the shoulder and making certain it is firm against the muscles.

into the shoulder firmly, and you will lean slightly forward to better absorb the recoil and to be prepared to move if necessary.

The grip on the fore-end and pistol grip is vital. The grip must be firm. I have seen fore-ends leap out of shooters' hands when firing 12-gauge buckshot. Be certain the support hand grasps the fore-end properly in its middle. This is especially important to smooth operation of a pump-action shotgun, but having this arm too far forward or too near the receiver on any shot-

This stance is okay for some users, but a more aggressive stance, one leaning into the gun, is more advantageous.

gun can compromise your handling of the shotgun and upset your overall balance. The best way to gauge the firing grip is to grasp the shotgun until the hands tremble, then back off a little and you have your firing grip.

When quickly shouldering the shotgun, both hands together on the gun, raise the shotgun to the shoulder and lean forward a bit at the same time. The emphasis here is on the word "together." Too much trigger hand raises the stock to the shoulder quickly, but the muzzle end is left behind. You are then more likely to overcompensate in bringing the muzzle to bear on the target, rising over it and having to bring it back down. Likewise with too much fore-end hand. In that case, the muzzle will be well above the target line when you set the gun into your shoulder and you'll have to bring the muzzle down and in line before you can shoot. Either fault wastes time and energy.

Another thing to keep in mind is that when mounting the shotgun, the shotgun is brought up and to the head and the cheek. You should not lower the head to meet the shotgun, you should not duck your head so that your shoulders come up around your ears. If the head is not properly aligned and upright, blood flow will be diminished and vision will blur, and when you scrunch your head down between your shoulders, you also lose awareness of your surroundings because you compromise your peripheral vision.

FIRST THINGS FIRST

What follows may sound very basic, especially if you've already spent some time on the range firing, but the goal here is to develop a strong, consistent set of gun handling skills that, in time, should become second nature. You need that to help overcome the extreme stress that will be present in a life-and-death situation and make decisions that can save your life.

Set a target with some sort of centered bull's-eye at a reasonable self-defense distance, 10 to 15 yards. From the firing line, fully load your shotgun with No. 7½ birdshot (it's cheap and easy on the shoulder for longer practice sessions). Focus on the bull's-eye, mount the shotgun to your shoulder, and fire.

The mounting and firing should be done in one smooth, fairly fast movement, but if you're new to this and find you've, say, impacted the top of the target, slow down. Speed comes from slow with this sort of thing, so repeat until you get this simple, repetitive set of motions right and are squarely impacting the target center mass every time you mount the shotgun. Getting accurate hits with single shots? Step it up. Advance to taking two shots with every shouldering of the shotgun.

This drill stresses the importance of making the first shot count, but also helps prepare you for an immediate second shot. It isn't about drills or working through scenarios at this point. You are simply becoming familiar with the operation and performance of the shotgun. You are learning to quickly get the shotgun into action and to aim correctly and fire with effect. Once you're good at that, change your distance to the target and start again. Mix it up with different targets, too, and then taking aim from kneeling and prone positions and from behind a barricade prop as you advance and improve.

Firing from below eye level is a viable tactic at very close range.

Consider that your attacker may be firing at you from behind their own cover. This is when knowing your shotgun well is a great advantage. If the threat is behind cover and only partially exposed, there is a good chance

Skill-Sharpening Drills

Once you have advanced from familiarity to competence with the shotgun, you will want to advance to combat-oriented drills. The following are designed to build confidence, control, and combat readiness.

When practicing range drills, it is a good idea to include topping off your magazine in the middle of your shooting strings.

Drill 1: Practice firing five shells, in three separate strings of fire, one string each at seven, 10, and 15 yards, and incorporating at least one combat (top-off) reload into the program.

Drill 2: Alternate firing twice at seven yards and twice at 15 yards. This drill can be augmented by performing a top-off reload with slugs for the 15-yard shots.

Speed is important in close-range drills, but so is accuracy.

Positive and aggressive action is needed to actuate the shotgun and handle recoil.

that part of the shot load will miss the adversary. Know your pattern and whether the shotgun fires high or low or to the left or right. Understand that firing multiple shots may be necessary to stop a threat if the threat is behind cover.

Part of the point of repetitive drills like this is to make sure that you're either properly operating the pump's action or supporting the semi-auto so that the action can do its job properly. If you do not properly and positively work the action on a pump, there is a good chance you will experience a short-cycle. When this happens, the empty hull in the chamber may fail to eject, and the shell coming from the magazine may become trapped on the shell carrier. The same can happen with a semi-auto. Fail to firmly grip and shoulder the semi-auto as it cycles—they call this "limp wristing" with semi-auto handguns—and this same jam can result. Either way with either gun, this is bad news if you are in a gunfight. Not only are such jams difficult and time-consuming to clear, you'll have to take your eyes off the problem, something that can give an aggressor an advantage.

RELOADING SKILLS

Having your firearm "run dry"—shot until empty—is not ideal in a firefight. That means you need to count your shots and reload before the gun is empty if the opportunity to do so presents itself. For instance, say you're fully loaded with six shells (five in the magazine, one in the chamber), and engaging an assailant who's invaded your place of shelter. You've fired two shots in response to a deadly threat by that assailant, but the assailant is either not hit or not hit enough and ducks into an adjoining room. If you've planned for such a situation, thought about how such a scenario could unfold, you should have a supply of ammunition at hand (in a drawer, in a pocket, on your shotgun's side-saddle shell carrier, on your ammo belt, etc.)—and *now* would be the time to "top off" and bring your shotgun back to full capacity. Now, before that assailant makes a reappearance with a friend or more firepower or anything that gives him an advantage over you.

There is an adage that if something needs shooting, it needs shooting twice. Keep the front sight on target and practice rapid fire.

Practicing reloading when you're relaxed is easy, but surprisingly, and if you've thought out your resupply, reloading with the gun on the shoulder is also easy and fast and offers two distinct advantages in a gunfight. First, it keeps the gun pointed in the direction of the threat and your eyes focused on that threat. Second, it allows you to quickly switch from buckshot to slugs or vice-versa as a situation evolves, all while saving precious time a reload with a dismounted gun involves and the inherent vulnerability to which that exposes you.

Practice the transition from buckshot to slugs during your range drills.

Practice loading the shotgun until you can do so with your eyes closed.

Leaving the gun on your shoulder and supported with your fore-end arm—and without taking your eyes off the target—quickly reach with your trigger hand for a shell from your resupply and seat it in the magazine. Repeat as you can until the gun is full. If danger were to reappear in the middle of this reload, the trigger hand could immediately return to the firing position (dropping a reload if necessary), and re-engage the assailant because the shotgun has remained in position.

More advanced shooters should practice this maneuver reversing hands and leaving the gun supported by the trigger hand. Certainly more difficult, it is possible for many with practice, when using a tactical shotgun that has a short, 18-inch barrel. You can also practice this reverse-hand reload from behind a barricade, with the barrel resting on top of the barricade. Either way, it can improve your ability to react to a given situation.

Of course, reloading before you run your gun dry may not be an option in a gunfight. Maybe your reload supply isn't immediately handy. Maybe the firefight has just been that intense. Maybe you're having a magazine malfunction of some sort and shells won't feed into the chamber, leaving you with what is, essentially a single-shot shotgun.

All is not lost.

Semi-autos and some dual-action shotguns such as the TriStar Tec-12 and Benelli M3 will lock open on the last shot. When that happens, a shell may be taken off of your shell belt, your receiver shell carrier, or from another reserve, quickly dropped into the chamber, the bolt release depressed to quickly close the bolt and you're back in action. For the right-handed shooter, this can be done with the gun still on the shoulder, supported by the fore-arm hand and the reload being performed by the trigger hand. Left-handed shooters will be more challenged with this if they do not have a left-handed firearm. There are two choices: 1) maintain a shoulder weld when supporting the firearm with the trigger hand (your left) and reload with the right hand; or 2) support the gun with the fore-end hand (right hand) and reach over the top of the receiver to drop a shell in the chamber with your trigger hand (left hand). If you cannot perfect either of these reloading methods as a left-hand shooter with a right-hand shotgun, you will always have to at least partially dismount the gun, if not fully, to perform a reload.

This single-shell chamber reload is a faster way to get the shotgun back into action than by loading the magazine and racking the bolt. And it will take practice, practice, practice to make your reloads smooth, fast, and complete (complete, as in you didn't drop a shell during the reload and have to fish for another). As it is with simply raising the gun to your shoulder and shooting one shot, two shots, and more and getting a center hit every time, start slowly, get good at the slow, then speed things up as you improve.

YES, YOU CAN MISS

Despite a common misconception, aiming a shotgun at very close range is just as important as aiming with a rifle. This is because the pattern hasn't spread yet and the payload must be centered for immediate effect. Use the sights or front bead to aim. Trigger control is also important. When you are swinging and firing, jerking the trigger will result in a wide miss. Practice smoothly pressing the trigger straight to the rear with targets at which you must aim. The trigger must be addressed consistently.

The tactical or combat-oriented shotgun is intended for engagements of short duration at close range. While the range of the shotgun may be stretched using slugs, the best range for a short-barreled tactical shotgun using buckshot or slugs is from seven to 30 yards. (The quality of the shotgun's sights will mean a great deal past this conversational range, and the skill of the user will become more important.)

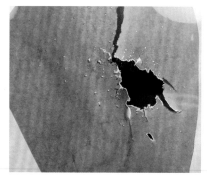

This is a shot from Federal's Personal Defense buckshot load at four yards. The tight group should amply explain just why it's possible to miss with a shotgun.

Taking Stock

A word about stock design as it relates to obtaining accurate hits with your tactical shotgun. When firing the shotgun quickly, the shotgun with a traditional stock works best for me and most others, because it's the easiest to swing due the hands' position on the gun. The pistol grip and AR-15-type stocks provide commonality of fit with companion AR-15 rifles, but their designs affect the ability to swing quickly and make smooth hits on running targets. I would advise that a great deal of practice must go into mastering the shotgun modified with an AR-15-style stock.

Let's look at that seven- to 30-yard range a different way as it relates to the tactical shotgun. Trainers refer to the three ranges of the shotgun as the A, B, and C ranges. At the A range, the pattern is still tight and cohesive and the shotgun must be aimed carefully. The B range is the range at which the pattern has spread but is still effective, usually about 15 to 20 yards. The C range is slug range, usually regarded as past 25 yards (although slugs may of course be used at closer range if needed). Remember the patterning discussion in Chapter 3? Well, that pattern "gives up" at a certain range and either is no longer dense enough or contains enough velocity to produce an aggression-stopping hit.

SHOOTING AND MOVING

If in a dire life-or-death scenario, it's conceivable that you will have to move at some point. Perhaps you were assailed in one part of your shelter but have an opportunity to move to a different room that offers more protection or a defensive advantage to you. Or maybe you're engaged in a defensive shooting and need to continue that defense while you move to your supply of ammunition or need to cut off an aggressor attacking family members in a different location.

Shooting, moving, and then shooting again is an advanced skill. Remember the saying "You have to walk before you run." Same goes for shooting. You have to be accomplished shooting while standing still before you can shoot after or during movement.

When moving, it is important to maintain your balance.

Hollywood makes shooting on the run look easy. It's not, but it can be done when you have all your shooting skill basics soundly in place and perfected. If you're getting accurate hits at combat distances and feel you're ready to add movement to your training, the place to start is to move *without* shooting. Shoot, assume the high-ready position of carry, with your finger off the trigger. ("High-ready" is simply carrying the shotgun upright with the muzzle about nose level and pointed up and away from your body.) Move to the next shooting position and shoulder the gun in preparation for your next shot.

Firing and moving should be practiced, but slowly at first. Safety—finger off the trigger, being aware of your surroundings, and avoiding things that may cause you to fall (including your own feet)—comes first. Speed will follow.

Start slowly with this training. Walk, don't run. Concentrate on how you transport the gun in between shooting positions and how fast you can reestablish the gun mount and accurately address the next target. When you are comfortable walking between shooting positions and your target reengagement hits after moving are accurate, move up to a jog and eventually run. Your heart rate and breathing will accelerate, adding another challenge to obtaining an accurate shot.

High-ready is a position that should be practiced when moving from one shooting location to another.

Moving *while* shooting is a very advanced skill. It is more technical than I can cover in this book, so my advice is for you to seek out a tactical instructor who teaches these skills. The basics, however, are this:

The gun will remain shouldered. Keep the muzzle of the shotgun facing the target and move carefully as you approach, back away from, or move sideways, shooting as you move. *Never* cross your feet while moving to prevent tripping yourself—in a real life-threatening situation your adrenaline

The shotgun should be tucked in when moving. Do not lead with the barrel, especially when going around a barricade corner, as someone may be on the other side ready to grab the shotgun.

Low-ready is easily maintained for long periods and useful for tasks like guard duty.

Relentless drills make for a formidable shooter.

will be high and this could easily happen. You'll need to maintain a solid grip on your shotgun and its position in your shoulder, a hard focus on the threat, and an awareness of your surroundings, including other potential threats, obstacles to your movement, and innocent bystanders both around you and behind your attacker. Again, start slowly and keep safety first and foremost in your mind.

TAKING ON MOVING TARGETS

A great aid to learning the shotgun is through sporting clays competition. This type of clay bird games pays dividends in rapid handling, target distance assessment, and required lead (how much in front of the target your muzzle has to be to connect with a distant moving target), and second-shot reaction. It isn't combat shooting at all, but it certainly teaches fast handling and accuracy. Of course, if the emergency situation you've prepared for dictates you'll need to hunt for your dinner, it isn't hard to see where sporting clays can help. Let's take a closer look at what this game entails.

Sporting clays are set on courses, much like a golf course. You'll shoot several targets from different "stands," moving from one stand to another throughout the course. A practice shoot usually consists of firing fifty rounds, and you'll use birdshot or comparable target loads in Nos. 9, 8, and 7½ shot.

There are several different clay "birds" you'll encounter in a sporting clays course. The standard clay dome is the same one thrown in the games of skeet and trap (also good general shotgun practice). A "midi" is slightly smaller, and the "mini" smaller yet. There's also a "battue" a rather flat disc that arcs in flight, and a "rabbit" that is thrown to bounce along the ground.

The clay birds may be thrown in a various ways at each station. You can have:

- A single bird.
- A report pair, in which a second bird is launched after you shoot the first one.
- A simultaneous pair, in which two birds are launched at one time and you'll have to choose which one to shoot first.

Also, pairs can be thrown with a mix of clay bird types and from different machines and directions.

To be successful at sporting clays and other clay bird games, you'll need to understand the three methods of establishing the lead I mentioned above. Remember how I said in an earlier chapter that with moving targets, you're shooting where the target is going to be, because you have to give the shot string time to get to the target. In other words, you have to anticipate where the target is going and time your trigger pull so that your pattern intercepts that point. There are three methods of doing this:

1. Pull-Through—You will mount the gun and insert the front bead/muzzle with the target's flight line *behind* the target, accelerating the swing so that your muzzle passes through the target before you pull the trigger ahead of it at the distance you feel is adequate to connect.
2. Pull-Away—You will mount the gun and insert the front bead/muzzle *on* the target, accelerating the swing so that your muzzle pulls away from the target before you pull the trigger ahead of it at the distance you feel is adequate to connect.
3. Maintained Lead—With maintained lead, you'll mount the gun and insert the front bead/muzzle in *front* of the target at the distance you feel is adequate to connect, then maintain the lead briefly before pulling the trigger.

    This is the more difficult of the three methods, for two reasons. First, the clay bird is always decelerating in flight, while live birds will mostly be accelerating, and you must match the pace of your swing to the target as you maintain the lead. Second, you have to shoot thousands of targets at dozens, even hundreds of distances before you "know" what the lead is for any given target.

With the other two methods, once you've practiced them for a while and learned about target connections, you tend to automatically swing with enough speed and to the point out in front of the target that makes the connection. This is just simple hand-eye coordination, much like how you learned to catch a baseball at some point, and once you become a more skilled shot, your movements are more automatic and instinctive. Maintaining a lead requires a richer bank of "I've shot this target at this distance before" memories in order to consistently connect, and that knowledge bank only comes from lots and lots of shooting at lots and lots of different targets.

As I've explained in a previous chapter, firing at a moving target is much different than standing and firing at a one-dimensional target squared to the shooter. When firing at moving targets, you must retain a hard visual focus on the target, *not* the front bead. You will shoot where you look, and if you are looking at your shotgun's bead, it's guaranteed you'll miss your target.

COMBAT GAMES

While clay bird games can help put food on the table in the event the world goes off-grid, it's the action shooting sport of 3-Gun that will boost your combat and self-defense skills. In 3-Gun, you'll also be required to shoot a handgun and rifle (which will likely also be part of your preparedness kit, so nothing wrong there), but it's how the game is played that makes the difference.

Like sporting clays, 3-Gun matches take place on a course. There will be multiple stages of fire. Some will utilize a single gun, others require switching guns within the stage. There is often lots of running, and you'll experience using cover, barricades, shooting from elevated positions, and more, all while engaging paper targets both static and moving, "hostage" targets, steel plates and more. There are even night shoots with tracer ammo, lasers, and lights, and some shoots have included the use of full-auto firearms loaned to the event by a sponsor. The sky's the limit, but the gist of the game is *defensive* shooting.

Firing from cover is a skill that should be part of your practice routine once you become more advanced.

The author is behind cover on the right and barely visible. Shooting from behind a barricade helps you overcome awkward shooting positions and compromised visibility to your target.

These are two fast hits with Federal buckshot.

Quickly moving to cover and understanding how cover shields a shooter can be crucial in a life-or-death situation.

Rapidly addressing multiple targets at close range is a difficult task. Swinging between close-range targets is actually more difficult than addressing targets at 20 yards or more.

Truly, 3-Gun can be an absolute hoot, but when you approach the game with the mindset of perfecting your firearms handling skills set for self-defense, then this competition becomes the ultimate training ground.

DAMAGE CONTROL

I've talked several times about the issue of short-cycling. This mostly occurs via user error with pump-actions, but an infirm hold on a semi-auto (limp-wristing) can produce the same problem. With an empty hull lodged in your ejection port and/or the next round failing to feed into the chamber, it doesn't take much to figure out how compromised you can be if you're in a fight for your life, but here's one example.

From my days in law enforcement, I remember that, during a particularly hot chase and gunfight, a state trooper was killed by dangerous felons when he experienced a short-cycle with his shotgun. He could have ended their career, but they lived another twenty-four hours or so before finally falling.

A short-cycle can happen to anyone. The surest way to prevent one is to keep the shotgun in the shoulder and manipulate the action firmly and aggressively on a pump, or maintain a firm grip and move with the gun during recoil with a semi-auto.

You may never have had one in practice, but remember that a fight for your life is going to be a nerve-wracking, terrifying experience. That's when the short-cycle could crop up for the first time, and you need to be ready to remedy it.

The best way I know to train for a short-cycle is to make it happen. Deliberately short-cycle the gun in practice and produce the jam. The only remedy to the jam I have seen that works with any speed is to kneel with the muzzle upwards and slam the butt of the shotgun to the ground. This forces the bolt to the rear and opens the action. This may also work with a semi-auto if you are unable to force the bolt back via its handle. Next, for the pump, ram the fore-end forward to load the chamber (for the semi-auto, hit the bolt release button). There are cases in which doing this to the pump may cause the action bars to be damaged, so you may not want to be too forceful during practice. If that damage occurs in a real self-defense situation, though, you'll need to go with what you know.

Another malfunction occurs when two shells jump the carrier and shell stop and try to load simultaneously. A drill that works with this malfunction in a pump is to run your finger into the carrier and press the lower shell back into the magazine. If one shell is behind the other, then the shell that is to the rear may be used to press the other shell into the magazine. A double feed malfunction in the self-loader above the elevator is sometimes easier to clear. Simply hold the bolt open and shake the shells out of the receiver opening. A double feed in the shell carrier is addressed in the same manner as with the pump shotgun.

A failure to feed or eject is usually something that occurs in a semi-auto, though a broken extractor in a pump can cause a failure of extraction too. There's really not a way to replicate this malfunction in practice, but you can practice the remedy. Load a single expended hull (not a live round) in the receiver only (none in the magazine), and simply treat the gun as if it's a single-shot. Rack the pump to open the bolt on a pump or pull the bolt lever to the rear on the semi-auto. If you've loaded the empty hull correctly, the extractor won't be around its rim and it will still be there in the chamber where you put it. Reach in and remove the hull. If you only partially loaded the empty hull and the extractor did catch the rim, work the slide rearward or the pull the bolt lever back a bit slowly, reaching for the hull to remove it from the receiver opening before the extractor kicks it out. Drop the hull—

Drills that include dropping a shell directly into the chamber may solve a malfunction problem in a life-or-death situation. Practicing such exercises adds to your ability to deal with stressful situations.

drop it!—reach for a fresh live shell, drop it directly into the receiver, close the bolt, shoulder the gun, and take your shot. As with anything, start this drill slowly, building speed as you become familiar with the empty hull extraction and live reload.

THE MENTAL SIDE OF SELF-DEFENSE TRAINING

The thought of engaging an adversary in gunfire is a terrifying one to almost all of us. This is reasonable. No one in their right mind wishes to endure the pain and agony of interpersonal conflict. No one *wants* to shoot someone else. But we fear more the harm such an adversary can do to us, and so also wish to put up a defense against that aggressor. That's human nature. To that end, you've decided that you wish to use a firearm to defend you and your loved ones in the event that someone wishes to do you lethal harm and you're reading this book in preparation for an event you hope will never happen.

When it comes to shooting, confidence is everything. When you practice with the shotgun, you are building something from nothing. Good skills are gained through constant practice. You must maintain a hard focus on

Complete familiarity with the shotgun is acquired through frequent range work.

the success of your skills. Nearly all students are fearful of failure, and you, reading this book, are a student of the shotgun. As you appraise your skill level and knowledge, know that fighting the fear of failure is a good foundation for battling the fear of combat.

When bird hunting, a bird hit well falls dead and provides instant feedback as to the success of your shot. In personal defense and combat shooting, however, the adversary may not fall when hit. In fact, an attacker may not react immediately in any way you'd expect. The files from my years in law enforcement contain instances in which felons took more than one load of 00 buckshot at ranges of five to 10 yards and were not immediately stopped. Too, know that many of our street drugs began life as pharmaceutical pain killers. Those criminals intoxicated with these powerful drugs can often take a lot of punishment. Be prepared to lay in multiple shots if needed.

The rule of thumb in self-defense is that *you fire until the aggression against you has stopped.* For all sorts of reasons, including those legal, that means you do *not* empty every round in your gun into an attacker *unless it is absolutely necessary to stop their lethal attack on you.*

Still, you need to be prepared for a single hit not to be enough. Practice receiving recoil from your first shot and firing again and even a third time until you produce consistent accuracy with each shot. Then advance your skills by engaging multiple targets. With such training and eventual success, you'll build the confidence necessary for you to react appropriately and rationally in a life-or-death situation.

CHAPTER 15

SHOTGUN MAINTENANCE

The least demanding of maintenance are the double-barrel shotguns, followed by pump-actions. The self-loader demands more frequent cleaning and lubrication. Regardless, a properly maintained shotgun isn't likely to malfunction. In most cases, shotguns that do malfunction are the ones that have been either abused or have not been cleaned and lubricated as they should have been—but in a life-and-death situation, your

These O rings will keep a shotgun such as the Remington 1100 going for many years.

health and welfare and that of your family may hinge upon the reliability of the shotgun. That means you need to care for yours properly.

WHAT TO EXPECT

It is true that some shotguns can operate for decades with little maintenance. After all, all we have in most cases is a plastic wad or sabot going down a smooth bore. Plastic fouling will accumulate and eventually affect performance, but there won't be the lead or copper fouling you'll find in rifles and handguns (except for when using full-bore rifle slugs lacking a sabot, of course). You will find powder residue, sometimes a lot depending on how clean the powder in the load was, and this can work its way into places it shouldn't. In semi-autos, there's also carbon fouling from the expended gases used to operate their actions, which absolutely will affect functionality.

When any type of shell or cartridge fires, there is a certain amount of primer compound and powder ash left in the firearm. As just stated, there may be lead from slugs and there is also some plastic left from wads and sabots. There are many good quality cleaning items that will wash the firearm clean of these residues.

Among the best products for shotgun barrel cleaning is the BoreSnake. This is simply a long, cloth tube with soft copper bristles embedded it. Sold by Hoppes 9 and available through most retailers and even on Amazon, the BoreSnake has a long string and a weighted tab at one end. Feed that end down the barrel of your unloaded gun, grasp it at the other end and pull the cleaning portion if the BoreSnake through. Two or three passes usually does

the trick, and you should see a mirror-shiny bore when you're finished.

Rifled barrels set up for slugs demand more care, and slug accuracy will deteriorate if you do not keep the barrel clean. While I prefer the BoreSnake for most shotgun barrel cleaning, for a rifled bore you're going to need a cleaning rod, copper brush in the right gauge size, and some lead or copper solvent to remove the lead and copper residue buildup from the barrel's rifling.

Your shotgun's barrel isn't the only thing that needs attention. You must also scrub the bolt and bolt face and remove any powder ash build-up under the extractor. Toothbrushes, cotton swabs, patches and a little cleaning solvent usually do the trick.

Gas-operated self-loading shotguns demand additional cleaning of their operating mechanisms to remove expended powder and carbon gas residues, some of which will have adhered to lubricant previously applied. Harder caked-on powder ash will have to be scrubbed with a soft toothbrush.

The Remington 1100 semi-auto demands proper lubrication. Given this care, it is incredibly reliable.

Keep the automatic shotgun properly lubricated and it will not fail you.

Inspect the working parts while you're cleaning them. Occasionally, "O" rings and some springs necessary to cycling the action will need to be replaced. Brownells.com and Midway.com are good resources for these replacement parts, as is the shotgun's manufacturer.

I actually keep a reasonable number of common replacement parts for my shotguns on hand. For example, I recently replaced the "O" ring on my 1980s-era Remington 1100 not because of a malfunction, but because it looked well-worn. Better to head off a problem than work with a failure.

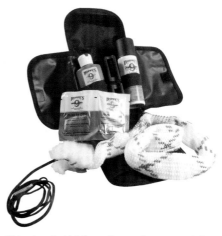

This cleaning kit from Brownells.com contains everything you need to clean your shotgun.

You do not have to clean your shotgun the way I do, but the procedure I follow has kept some of my shotguns going for a long time.

Start with an unloaded gun and no ammo anywhere in your cleaning area. Next, you need to know how to field-strip the shotgun. This usually means removing the barrel and bolt (or just the barrels on a double-barrel). You do not have to learn how to detail strip the trigger action, but it would be helpful. Your owner's manual will explain how to do both and, more important, tell you what *not* to take apart.

From Brownells.com, this BoreSnake makes barrel cleaning a cinch.

After cleaning inside of the barrel with the BoreSnake (and brush as needed), and after scrubbing

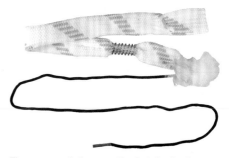

There are variations on the BoreSnake for each gauge.

and wiping away other dirt buildup from gas actions and bolts, lubricate the long bearing surfaces that have metal-to-metal contact. No need to have them dripping with lube, just enough to keep things working nicely together. Also, be wary of getting lube inside the bolt face and anywhere wood meets metal. Lube will seep into wood and discolor, even soften it. Once done, simply reassemble the firearm. Finally, wipe the outer metal parts down with a lightly oiled cloth or one of the chemically impregnated cloths meant for this purpose to remove fingerprints, dirt, and any excess oil from your lubrication of other parts. This goes a long way toward forestalling rust.

Use only cleaning products and lubes designed for use with firearms. Kerosene, brake cleaner, and WD40 have been used by some in the past, but they aren't good for either your gun or you.

Don't be stingy with lubricant! Shotguns may run dirty but not dry.

If you use the Adaptive Tactical Wraptor fore-end or other accessories, be certain all screws are tight at the end of your maintenance session.

DON'T FORGET YOUR SCREW-IN CHOKES

The screw-in shotgun choke also requires problem cleaning and maintenance, especially as this is where a lack of maintenance may result in injury or expensive firearm repairs. You'll see excessive plastic buildup on the interior and their threads tend accumulate a lot of grit and carbon residue. These threads are fine and thin, and just a little powder ash or a few grains of powder can cause problems when inserting and removing. When you screw the choke tube in, the tube must seat firmly on a small shelf inside the barrel. If there is any space between the tube and this shelf, then material may wedge in and create a buildup. If fouling becomes trapped between the choke tube and this gap, you will have a dangerous situation.

Choke tubes may become caked with powder and plastic and present a problem with fit and function and can pose a safety problem.

The choke tube sometimes becomes stuck in the barrel, and the wad and shot roaring down the barrel may catch a portion of the choke tube bottom and split the tube and the barrel. That's what's called a catastrophic failure, and besides ruining your gun, it can cause bodily injury to you and bystanders.